World War II
Book of Lists

World War II
Book of Lists
Chris Martin

To my Dad, who knows more about
this subject that I ever will.

Cover illustration: 1940s USA army supplies poster. (The Advertising Archives)

First published 2011

The History Press
The Mill, Brimscombe Port
Stroud, Gloucestershire, GL5 2QG
www.thehistorypress.co.uk

British Library Cataloguing in Publication Data.
A catalogue record for this book is available from the British Library.

ISBN 978 0 7524 6163 2

Typesetting and origination by The History Press
Printed in Great Britain

Book of Lists

The statesman who yields to war fever must realise that once the signal is given, he is no longer the master of policy but the slave of unforeseeable and uncontrollable events.

Sir Winston Churchill

The Second World War was the first truly modern conflict – a total war in which few were left untouched. It saw the deaths of between 50 and 70 million people worldwide, and remains the largest and most destructive conflict our planet has ever seen.

Unlike the First World War, which had been largely contained by brutal trench warfare in northern Europe, the Second World War was an intensely mobile affair which was played out over a vast area. From the jungles of Borneo to the icy wastes of the Russian steppes, advances in mechanisation, transport and communications allowed men to fight on land, sea and air, and in all weather conditions. In addition to the movement of military forces, long-range bombing raids and lightning-fast invasions brought death and destruction to peoples' doorsteps, seeing a blurring of the lines between combatants and civilians that was unprecedented.

To give an idea of the huge scope of the war: in the six years between 1939 and 1945 ninety-two countries would become involved, to some degree or another, in the fighting. While a few of these did manage to remain untouched by the mayhem, many would end up engaging the bulk of their military and industrial might in a concerted effort to destroy their enemies.

This book does not aim to be a comprehensive history of those tumultuous years, instead it gathers together facts, figures, quotations and stories to create a snapshot of the life during the war. Here we have collected a selection of the key military events of those dramatic years, as well as the weapons and vehicles that were used in the field, and stories of exceptional valour among combatants on all sides. There are details of some of the incredible scientific and technological advances involved in the struggle for dominance: from complex code machines and life-saving medical procedures to sophisticated weapons and the dawn of the atomic age. You will also find some of the minutiae from the everyday lives of those involved: what was worn into battle, what was eaten at home and even the entertainment that provided a welcome distraction from the carnage.

Finally, if this book has one purpose, it is to once again draw attention to the debt of gratitude we all owe to the grit, resilience and courage of those who lived and died, both at home and abroad, to make our world a better, more peaceful place.

Squaring Up – The Allies and Axis Forces

The Second World War had two primary opposing forces – the Allies and the Axis:

 The Allies – Led by the 'Big Three' superpowers: the Union of Soviet Socialist Republics (USSR, or the Soviet Union), the United States of America and Great Britain. Those countries which formed Great Britain's empire entered the war with them as Crown colonies (for example, India), whereas other semi-independent members of the British Commonwealth, known as the Dominions, declared war on Germany separately (for example Australia, Canada and South Africa). The Allies were also aligned with France, Belgium, the Netherlands, Greece, Norway, Yugoslavia, Czechoslovakia, Ethiopia, New Zealand, Brazil, Mexico and China.

The Axis – Also know as the Axis Alliance, Axis nations or Axis countries, it consisted of Germany, Italy and Japan. The Axis was formed by two key treaties which united their military ambitions: the 'Pact of Steel' between Germany and Italy in 1939, and the 'Tripartite Pact' between Germany, Italy and Japan in 1940. The Axis was also aligned with Hungary, Romania, Bulgaria and Finland. During the course of the war the Axis powers created puppet or collaborating states in the countries they invaded (for example Vichy France) who also declared war on the Allies.

Across the course of the war the combatants fought in four major areas:

A trio of regions in the West loosely grouped as the European Theatre, consisting of the Western Front (which covered Western Europe), the Eastern Front (which covered Eastern Europe and Russia) and the Mediterranean (which included North Africa). The European Theatre was an area of heavy fighting from 1 September 1939 through to 8 May 1945.

In the East the conflict spread across most of the Pacific. The Pacific Theatre consisted of Asia, Japan and the Pacific islands. This area saw heavy conflict between 1942 and 1945 and spread across most of the Pacific, but excluded some key territories in the area such as Australia and the Dutch East Indies.

Declarations of War

The history books record that the war began with British opposition to the invasion of Poland by Nazi Germany. In fact, this was just the touch paper for a global explosion of long-held territorial and ideological conflicts, which then spread uncontrollably across the world. In the ensuing chaos, even those nations who were not disposed to fight were drawn into the mayhem, either by their alliances, the need to defend themselves, or invasion. Here are the declarations by year:

1939

3 September	Great Britain declares war on Germany.
6 September	The Union of South Africa declares war on Germany.
10 September	Canada declares war on Germany.

1940

8 April	Norway declares war on Germany.
10 June	Italy declares war on Great Britain and France.
11 June	France declares war on Italy.
23 November	Belgium declares war on Italy.

1941

6 April	Italy declares war on Yugoslavia.
24 April	Bulgaria declares war on Greece, Hungary and Yugoslavia.
26 June	Finland declares war on the Soviet Union.

27 June	Hungary declares war on the Soviet Union.
7 December	Great Britain, Australia and New Zealand declare war on Finland, Hungary and Romania.
	Canada declares war on Finland, Hungary, Japan and Romania.
	Panama declares war on Japan.
8 December	Great Britain declares war on Japan.
	The United States declares war on Japan.
	Japan declares war on the United States, Great Britain, Australia, Canada, New Zealand and the Union of South Africa.
	The Union of South Africa declares war on Finland, Hungary, Japan and Romania.
	Australia, Costa Rica, the Dominican Republic, El Salvador, Haiti, Honduras, the Netherlands, New Zealand and Nicaragua declare war on Japan.
	The Free French National Council declares war on Germany.
	Manchukuo declares war on the United States.
9 December	China declares war on Germany, Italy and Japan.
	Cuba and Guatemala declare war on Japan.
11 December	The United States declares war on Germany and Italy.
	Costa Rica, Cuba, the Dominican Republic, Guatemala and Nicaragua declare war on Germany.
	Germany and Italy declare war on the United States.
	The Netherlands declares war on Italy.
	Poland declares war on Japan.
12 December	Romania declares war on the United States.
13 December	Great Britain, New Zealand and the Union of South Africa declare war on Bulgaria.

Honduras declares war on Germany and Italy.
Italy declares war on Cuba and Guatemala.

14 December   Croatia declares war on the United States.

16 December   Czechoslovakia declares war on all countries at war with the United States, Great Britain and the Soviet Union.

17 December   Albania declares war on the United States.

19 December   Nicaragua declares war on Bulgaria, Hungary and Romania.

20 December   Belgium declares war on Japan.

24 December   Haiti declares war on Bulgaria, Hungary and Romania.

1942

6 January   Australia declares war on Bulgaria.

11 January   Japan declares war on the Netherlands.

25 January   Thailand declares war on the United States and Great Britain.

22 March   Australia declares war on Thailand.

22 May   Mexico declares war on Germany, Italy and Japan.

5 June   The United States declares war on Bulgaria, Hungary and Romania.

22 August   Brazil declares war on Germany and Italy.

14 December   Ethiopia declares war on Germany, Italy and Japan.

1943

17 January   Iraq declares war on Germany, Italy and Japan.

7 April   Bolivia declares war on the Axis powers.

1 August   Burma declares war on Great Britain and the United States.

9 September   Iran declares war on Germany.

13 October	Italy declares war on Germany.
4 December	The Bolivian Cabinet declares war on the Axis powers.

1944

27 January	Liberia declares war on Germany and Japan.
27 March	Argentina declares war on Germany and Japan.
25 August	Romania declares war on Germany.
5 September	The Soviet Union declares war on Bulgaria.
7 September	Hungary declares war on Romania.
	Romania declares war on Hungary.
21 September	San Marino declares war on Germany.

1945

20 January	Hungary declares war on Germany.
7 February	Paraguay declares war on Germany and Japan.
23 February	Turkey declares war on Germany and Japan.
24 February	Egypt declares war on Germany and Japan.
26 February	Syria declares war on Germany and Japan.
27 February	Lebanon declares war on Germany and Japan.
1 March	Iran declares war on Japan.
	Saudi Arabia declares war on Japan.
3 March	Finland declares war on Germany.
7 March	Romania declares war on Japan.
11 April	Chile declares war on Japan.
6 June	Brazil declares war on Japan.
6 July	Norway announces that it declared war on Japan on 7 December 1941.
14 July	Italy declares war on Japan.
8 August	The Soviet Union declares war on Japan.
9 August	Mongolia declares war on Japan.

Feeding the Forces – Red Cross Food Parcels

By the end of the war, over 20 million food parcels had been sent to British prisoners of war by the Joint War Organisation of the British Red Cross and Order of St John of Jerusalem. The contents of these parcels were carefully chosen to supplement the food and personal supplies available to those incarcerated in prison camps, and were usually sent at the rate of one per man per week. They contained the following items:

- ¼lb packet of tea
- 1 tin of cocoa powder
- 1 bar of milk or plain chocolate
- 1 tinned pudding
- 1 tin of meat roll
- 1 tin of processed cheese
- 1 tin of condensed milk
- 1 tin of dried eggs
- 1 tin of sardines or herrings
- 1 tin of preserves
- 1 tin of margarine
- 1 tin of sugar
- 1 tin of vegetables
- 1 tin of biscuits

 1 bar of soap

 1 tin of 50 cigarettes or tobacco (sent separately)

Top Ten Flying Aces – Chocs Away

The ultimate measure of a wartime pilot's courage and skill was the number of confirmed kills he could claim. The opportunity to engage the enemy, the performance of the aircraft he flew and the quality of his opposition were all contributing factors to his final total. In the age before computer-assisted flying, often it was just down to a pilot's guts and expertise behind the joystick. Boosted by their massacre of the woefully unprepared and antiquated Soviet Air Force in 1941, it is perhaps not that surprising that Germany leads the pack by some considerable way when we tot up the scores:

Top Ten German Aces

Erich 'Bubi' Hartmann, Luftwaffe	352
Gerhard Barkhorn, Luftwaffe	301
Günther Rall, Luftwaffe	275
Otto Kittel, Luftwaffe	267
Walter 'Nowi' Nowotny, Luftwaffe	258
Wilhelm Batz, Luftwaffe	237
Erich Rudorffer, Luftwaffe	222

Heinz Bär, Luftwaffe	220
Hermann Graf, Luftwaffe	212
Heinrich Ehrler, Luftwaffe	208

Top Ten Soviet Aces

Ivan Kozhedub, Soviet Air Force	62
Aleksandr Ivanovich Pokryshkin, Soviet Air Force	59
Grigoriy Rechkalov, Soviet Air Force	58
Nikolay Gulayev, Soviet Air Force	57
Kirill Yevstigneyev, Soviet Air Force	53
Dmitriy Glinka, Soviet Air Force	50
Alexandru Şerbănescu, Romanian Air Force	47
Arseniy Vorozheikin, Soviet Air Force	46
Aleksandr Koldunov, Soviet Air Force	46
Nikolay Skomorohov, Soviet Air Force	46

Top Ten RAF Aces

Marmaduke 'Pat' Pattle, RAF (South Africa)	51+
James Edgar 'Johnnie' Johnson, RAF	38
Brendan Eamon Fergus 'Paddy' Finucane, RAF (Ireland)	32
Adolph 'Sailor' Malan, RAF (South Africa)	32
George F. Beurling, RAF (Canada)	31
William Vale, RAF	30+ (6 shared)
Robert Roland Stanford Tuck, RAF	29
Bob Braham, RAF	29
'Ginger' Lacey, RAF	28
Colin Falkland Gray, RAF (New Zealand)	27.5

Top Ten US Aces

Richard I. Bong, US Army Air Forces	40
Thomas B. McGuire, US Army Air Forces	38
David McCampbell, US Navy	34
Francis 'Gabby' Gabreski, US Army Air Forces	28

(+2.5 ground, +6.5 Korea)

Gregory 'Pappy' Boyington, US Marine Corps	28

(counting 6 with the AVG)

Robert S. Johnson, US Army Air Forces	27
Charles H. MacDonald, US Army Air Forces	27
George E. Preddy, Jnr, US Army Air Forces	26.83

(+5 ground)

Joseph J. Foss, US Marine Corps	26
John C. Meyer, US Army Air Forces	24

(+13 ground, +2 Korea)

 Top Ten Japanese Aces

Hiroyoshi Nishizawa, Imperial Japanese Navy	87
Tetsuzo Iwamoto, Imperial Japanese Navy	80–7
Ryotaro Jobou, Imperial Japanese Army	76
Shoichi Sugita, Imperial Japanese Navy	70
Saburo Sakai, Imperial Japanese Navy	64+
Hiromichi Shinohara, Imperial Japanese Army	58
Takeo Okumura, Imperial Japanese Navy	54
Satoru Anabuki, Imperial Japanese Navy	51
Yasuhiko Kuroe, Imperial Japanese Army	51
Iyozo Hujita, Imperial Japanese Navy	39

Wartime Lingo – Quotations from General George S. Patton

Of all the larger-than-life characters found in the annals of the war, none looms larger than the controversial and outspoken figure of George S. Patton. Forthright in conversation and audacious in battle, Patton was a career soldier who became a legend in his own wartime. Patton's frank demeanour was combined with pearl-handled pistols, riding breeches and outsized insignia, creating an image that made it clear he intended to lead his troops from the front all the way to Berlin.

As one United Press International (UPI) writer noted at the time: 'This absolute faith in himself as a strategist and master of daring infected his entire army, men of the second American corps in Africa, and later the third army in France, believed they could not be defeated under his leadership.' Below are just some of the quotes in which Patton summed up his hard-nosed attitude to warfare:

- 'No one ever won a war by dying for his country ... you win a war by making the other poor son of a bitch die for his.'
- 'I'd rather have the German army ahead of me than the French army behind me.'
- 'May God have mercy upon my enemies, because I won't.'
- 'Wars may be fought with weapons, but they are won by men.'
- 'The test of success is not what you do when you're on top. Success is how high you bounce when you hit bottom.'
- 'Never in history has the navy landed an army at the planned time and place. But if you land us anywhere within 50 miles of Fedela and within 1 week of D-Day, I'll go ahead and win.'
- 'Sure, we want to go home. We want this war over with. The quickest way to get it over with is to go get the bastards who started it.'

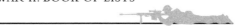

 'We can no more understand a Russian than a Chinese or a Japanese, and from what I have seen of them, I have no particular desire to understand them except to ascertain how much lead or iron it takes to kill them.'

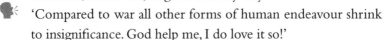 'Lead me, follow me, or get out of my way.'

'Compared to war all other forms of human endeavour shrink to insignificance. God help me, I do love it so!'

Fleeing the Storm – Neutral States

Throughout the war, several states remained neutral during the conflict. A neutral power is a sovereign state that declares itself to be neutral towards those other countries in conflict; a move designed to avoid invasion or to conform with a wider policy of neutrality in all diplomatic affairs. The following countries were assigned as neutral from the outbreak of fighting in 1939 and the end of hostilities in 1945:

- Afghanistan
- Estonia
- Latvia
- Lithuania
- North Yemen

- Ireland (Eire)
- Portugal
- Spain
- Sweden
- Switzerland
- Vatican City

In many cases, such a declaration did not mean the country was demilitarised. On the contrary, many of the nations which declared themselves neutral during the war did increase their armed forces in case they were required to defend their borders. A precaution which was amply supported by the German invasions of Belgium, Norway and the Netherlands, all of whom had declared themselves neutral at the start of hostilities.

Actors Who Have Played Winston Churchill

Before he led the country to victory, Winston Churchill had already led an amazing life as an aristocrat, politician, journalist and soldier. The larger than life character of the man and his extraordinary deeds have meant that actors have queued up to play the great man on the big and small screens ever since. Here are just ten of them:

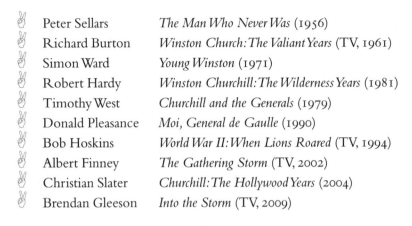

	Peter Sellars	*The Man Who Never Was* (1956)
	Richard Burton	*Winston Church: The Valiant Years* (TV, 1961)
	Simon Ward	*Young Winston* (1971)
	Robert Hardy	*Winston Churchill: The Wilderness Years* (1981)
	Timothy West	*Churchill and the Generals* (1979)
	Donald Pleasance	*Moi, General de Gaulle* (1990)
	Bob Hoskins	*World War II: When Lions Roared* (TV, 1994)
	Albert Finney	*The Gathering Storm* (TV, 2002)
	Christian Slater	*Churchill: The Hollywood Years* (2004)
	Brendan Gleeson	*Into the Storm* (TV, 2009)

Special Units – Merrill's Marauders

Led by Brigadier General Frank Merrill, Merrill's Marauders was the unofficial name given the 5307th Composite Unit, a long-range Special Forces unit which fought behind enemy lines in the Burma Campaign. The unit became famous for its deep-penetration missions against the Japanese; always outnumbered by hostile enemy forces and often trekking huge distances through some of the toughest terrain known to man. Here are a few facts about the unit:

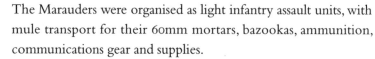

- The Marauders were organised as light infantry assault units, with mule transport for their 60mm mortars, bazookas, ammunition, communications gear and supplies.

- Designed to strike behind enemy lines where they were least expected, officers and men were trained to survive in the jungle and received instruction on scouting and patrolling, stream crossings, camouflage and the then innovative technique of supply by air-drop.

- Their training and the mental toughness it instilled paid off when, on 17 May 1944, after a gruelling 65-mile march over the 6,000ft Kumon mountain range fighting meagre rations and disease, approximately 1,300 Marauders successfully attacked an unsuspecting Japanese airfield at the Myitkyina.

- The men of the Merrill's Marauders have enjoyed the rare distinction of seeing every soldier who served with the unit awarded the Bronze Star.

- In June 1944, Merrill's Marauders were awarded the Distinguished Unit Citation. The report read: 'The unit must display such gallantry, determination, and *esprit de corps* in accomplishing its mission under extremely difficult and hazardous conditions as to set it apart and above other units participating in the same campaign.'

Five Greatest Tanks of the War

 T-34

The first T-34s rolled off the assembly line the KhPZ factory in Kharkov, Ukraine in 1940. Hardy and versatile, the Russian T-34 was the most produced tank of the war, and remains the second most produced tank of all time. The T-34 had a well-armoured shell, a good gun and was well served by its excellent cross-country mobility. But it is the sheer numbers in which it was produced that made it the tank that won the war on the Eastern Front. The simplicity and versatility of the design meant that in the Soviet Union's darkest years, these war machines could even be produced in makeshift workshops in the besieged Stalingrad.

Though T-34s were rugged, fast and reliable in the field, they did suffer from the economies taken to build them: the commander had to double as a gunner, while Soviet shortages meant crews were seldom well trained, and often went into action without basic provisions and essential items such as radios.

 M4 Sherman

Named following the American practice of christening their tanks after famous Civil War generals, the M4 Sherman was the backbone of almost all US army ground offensives from 1942. As well as the tens of thousands of M4s used by US forces, thousands more were distributed to the Allies on the Western and Eastern Fronts via the Lend-Lease programme.

The Sherman evolved from the Grant and Lee medium tanks, and it retained much of their mechanical design. However, the success of the Soviet T-34 on the Eastern

Front ensured that the Sherman's designers aimed to create a machine that shared the Russian tank's mechanical reliability and ease of production – the Sherman even used standardised parts and ammunition to aid maintenance in the field. One notable addition was a hefty 75mm gun mounted on a fully traversing gyrostabilised turret, which enabled its crew to fire while the tank was on the move.

The Sherman's reliability, and the fact that it could be easily adapted to carry a variety of different weapons, made it superior in many regards to the German light and medium tanks of the blitzkrieg. Yet the Sherman did have a fatal flaw: its fuel tank caught fire easily. It was this deadly trait that gave the Sherman a second nickname: the 'Zippo'.

 Panther

The Sd.Kfz. 171, more commonly known as the Panther, was a German medium tank in service from mid-1943 to the close of the European Theatre in 1945. Its combination of firepower, mobility and solid armour mean that it is regarded as one of the best tank designs of the war. The Panther was born from the recommendations of a special Panzerkommision, despatched to the Eastern Front to assess the success of the nimble T-34. As such, the Panther stole many of its strongest features from its rival: including rounded turret design, wide tracks to aid mobility over soft ground and sloping front armour to increase defence against shell penetration – indeed, the Panther had the same front armour as Tiger I.

This balance of armour and firepower was undermined by the German commitment to technological advance. The tank was full of new and often complex engineering that made it difficult to maintain in the field, notably its interleaved suspension and a hydraulics system which could be set on fire if hit. Regardless of these drawbacks, it remains one of the best individual feats of engineering in the war.

 ### Tiger/King Tiger

Though only a handful of them survive in museums worldwide, if most people were asked to name a single tank from the war they would say the fearsome Tiger. Tiger I was the common name given to the heavy tank designated by the Wehrmacht as the 'Panzerkampfwagen Tiger Ausf. E'. Deployed in 1942, it was developed as an answer to the unexpected strength of Soviet armour encountered in the initial months of Operation Barbarossa, particularly the T-34 and the KV-1. To counter this threat, the Tiger I gave the German forces their first tank mounted with a massive, tank-busting 88mm gun. Usually deployed in an independent tank battalion, the Tiger I saw combat – and struck fear into its enemies – on all German battlefronts during the course of the war. As a machine it was immensely heavy at 50 metric tons – the price for the 3.9ins of armour protecting its crew – and possessed the kind of sheer firepower that could prove decisive with a single shell.

Like many German tanks it was over-engineered as a vehicle. Expensive and time-consuming to produce, just 1,347 Tigers were built between August 1942 and August 1944. Furthermore, the Tiger, like the Panther, was prone to track failures which left these mighty beasts immobile, while its interlocking wheels made it complicated to transport without damaging it. In 1944 production was phased out in favour of the Tiger II.

PzKfW Mk. IV Panzer

The Mk. IV Panzer tank was introduced in 1937 and was used with devastating effectiveness in the German blitzkrieg attacks on Poland, France, the Low Countries and the Soviet Union. Weighing in at 17.6 tons with a fast-firing, short-barrelled 75mm gun, the Mk. IV was ideal for supporting infantry while its hull and turret-mounted machine guns could also destroy it. Initially, the frontal armour of the tank was just 30mm thick, which soon proved ineffective against the second generation Allied armour. As a result, later versions of the Mk. IV were produced with 50mm and 80mm armour. By far the most prolifically used German tank of the war between 1940 and 1945; some 9,000 of them rolled out of German factories.

Hollywood Goes to War – Movie Stars Who Served in Battle

Following the outbreak of war, many stars of the silver screen joined ordinary Joes to enlist in the Allied forces and serve their country. Well-known names like Clark Gable, Mickey Rooney and Carl Reiner were, by choice, for medical reasons or by the wisdom of their superiors, assigned to the production of propaganda documentaries and inspiring films to entertain the troops; some even found themselves

right in the heart of the action. Here is our list of the Hollywood hard men who played their part in combat during the war:

- **Ernest Borgnine** – Served in the US navy for ten years and aboard the destroyer USS *Lamberton* (DD-119) during the war. His military decorations included the American Campaign Medal, the Good Conduct Medal, the American Defence Service Medal with Fleet Clasp and the Second World War Victory Medal.
- **Charles Bronson** – Served in the US Army Air Forces as an aerial gunner in a B-29 Superfortress. He was awarded a Purple Heart for wounds he received during his service.
- **Tony Curtis** – Joined the US navy at the age of 17 where, as a crew member on the submarine USS *Proteus*, he watched the Japanese surrender ceremonies from the signal bridge of its tender.
- **Kirk Douglas** – Joined up with the US navy in 1941. He was medically discharged as a result of war injuries in 1944.
- **Douglas Fairbanks Jnr** – Served in the US navy both on the battleship *Massachusetts* and as a commando raider. He retired as a full captain.
- **Henry Fonda** – Enlisted in the US navy and served for three years: initially as a quartermaster on the destroyer USS *Satterlee* and later as a lieutenant in Air Combat Intelligence. He was awarded a Presidential Citation and the Bronze Star.
- **Lee Marvin** – Served with the US Marines as a scout sniper in the 4th Marine Division. He was wounded in action during the Second World War Battle of Saipan, during which most of his platoon was killed. He was awarded the Purple Heart.
- **David Niven** – Attended the officer training college at Sandhurst as a young man and served with the British army during the war; taking part in the invasion of Normandy as part of the 'Phantom Signals Unit', which located and reported enemy positions.

- **Rod Stieger** – Lied about his age to enlist in the US navy at the age of 16. He saw action on destroyers as a torpedo man in the Pacific.
- **Jimmy Stewart** – Joined the US Army Air Corps where he initially served as an instructor before being moved to active duty in 1943. He flew numerous bombing missions over Nazi Germany and twice received the Distinguished Flying Cross for actions in combat.

Wartime Lingo – Great Speeches

 'Never was so much owed by so many to so few …'
'Never was so much owed by so many to so few …' was a speech made by the British prime minister, Winston Churchill, on 20 August 1940 in the House of Commons. The speech sought to capture the gallantry of the Royal Air Force (RAF) who, while outnumbered three to one, had managed to repel an all-out attack by German Luftwaffe over the skies of southern England. Had the German air force defeated the RAF, the air assault would almost certainly have been followed by a full-scale ground invasion.

Inspired by a visit to the operations room at RAF Uxbridge the day after the pivotal air battle, Churchill sought to capture both his admiration for the hard-pressed – and often barely trained – pilots, but also the gratitude of the relieved nation:

The gratitude of every home in our Island, in our Empire, and indeed throughout the world, except in the abodes of the guilty, goes out to the British airmen who, undaunted by odds, unwearied in their constant challenge and mortal danger, are turning the tide of the World War by their prowess and by their devotion. Never in the field of human conflict was so much owed by so many to so few. All our hearts go out to the fighter pilots, whose brilliant actions we see with our own eyes day after day …

 'We shall fight them on the beaches …'
We Shall Fight on the Beaches is the title given to a speech delivered by Winston Churchill on 4 June 1940 in the House of Commons. The speech saw Churchill, who had been elected head of a multi-party coalition only a month earlier, make a definitive statement about British resolve to resist the terrifyingly fast spread of the German blitzkrieg.

At the time Churchill came to power, the German forces had already swept through the Netherlands, Belgium and Luxembourg. His speech was instigated by his government's very real fears that French military forces were about to collapse, leaving the British mainland open to an invasion attempt.

Ever the master of public speaking, Churchill used this talent for oratory to prepare the people of Britain for the peril the country faced and put them in no doubt that Great Britain would use all the resources in her power to resist Nazism:

We shall fight in France, we shall fight on the seas and oceans, we shall fight with growing confidence and growing strength in the air, we shall defend our island, whatever the cost may be. We shall fight on the beaches, we shall fight on

the landing grounds, we shall fight in the fields and in the streets, we shall fight
in the hills; we shall never surrender, and even if, which I do not for a moment
believe, this Island or a large part of it were subjugated and starving, then our
Empire beyond the seas, armed and guarded by the British Fleet, would carry
on the struggle, until, in God's good time, the new world, with all its power and
might, steps forth to the rescue and the liberation of the old.

'The Arsenal of Democracy'

'The Arsenal of Democracy' was a radio broadcast by President
Franklin D. Roosevelt on 29 December 1940, in which he
sought to reposition the war in Europe in the American mindset.
It marked a crucial turning point in US foreign policy, in which
it abandoned isolationism and chose to take critical role as a
world power. The speech saw Roosevelt promise to supply
the British and Russians with military equipment in order to
support their fight against the Axis, while staying – initially
anyway – out of the conflict. The commitment could not have
come at a more critical time. In the West, Nazi Germany had
occupied most of Europe and was expanding quickly into
Russia. In the East, Japan had swept through large areas of
British colonies following the collapse of the Commonwealth.

In the speech, Roosevelt referred to Detroit as 'the great
arsenal of democracy' because of the speed in which it had
repurposed much of its automotive industry to produce
armaments. Roosevelt said:

We must be the great arsenal of democracy. For us this is an emergency as
serious as war itself. We must apply ourselves to our task with the same
resolution, the same sense of urgency, the same spirit of patriotism and sacrifice
as we would show were we at war.

The 'Jewel Voice Broadcast'

Gyokuon-hōsō or the 'Jewel Voice Broadcast' was a pre-recorded phonograph broadcast by radio, in which Japanese Emperor Hirohito announced to his people the unconditional surrender of the Japanese government to the Allies. The speech was broadcast at noon on 15 August 1945 in both Japanese and English, and, while it is not a stirring piece of rhetoric, it marks the first time the divine Japanese emperor had ever spoken directly to his people.

The capitulation was prompted by Japan's losses at the Battle of Okinawa, the declaration of war against Japan by the Soviet Union and, most specifically, the dropping of the atomic bombs on Hiroshima and Nagasaki. Indeed, the emperor specifically referred to the cataclysmic effect of 'a new and most cruel bomb, the power of which to do damage is, indeed, incalculable ...'.

While most would not doubt the wisdom of the emperor's decision, the concept of surrender was so alien to Japanese culture at the time that as many as 1,000 military officers attempted to raid the Imperial palace the evening before the broadcast to destroy the recording. Emperor Hirohito said:

It is according to the dictates of time and fate that we have resolved to pave the way for a grand peace for all the generations to come by enduring the unendurable and suffering what is insufferable.

British High Command

- **Winston Churchill** (1874–1965) – A career politician, Churchill served as First Lord of the Admiralty, Home Secretary and Chancellor of the Exchequer before becoming Prime Minister from May 1940. He retired from politics in 1955.
- **Neville Chamberlain** (1869–1940) – Prime Minister from May 1937 until May 1940. His policy of appeasement of the Nazis lost him the confidence of the British people.
- **Clement Atlee** (1883–1967) – Deputy Prime Minister in Churchill's coalition government. He became Prime Minister following Churchill's defeat in the general election of July 1945, where he oversaw the decolonisation of much of the British Empire.
- **Anthony Eden** (1897–1977) – After briefly rejoining the army at the start of the war, Eden served in a variety of roles in the Churchill government; notably the Foreign Office, the Political Warfare Executive and as Leader of the House of Commons.
- **Field Marshal John Dill** (1881–1944) – Chief of the Imperial General Staff from May 1940 until December 1941. Thereafter he worked in Washington as the Senior British Representative on the Combined Chiefs of Staff building the 'special relationship' between the United Kingdom and the United States.
- **Field Marshal Alan Brooke** (1883–1963) – Chief of the Imperial General Staff during the war, promoted to field marshal in 1944. As chairman of the Chiefs of Staff Committee, he was the foremost military advisor to Churchill.
- **Air Chief Marshal Charles Portal** (1893–1971) – Appointed Chief of the Air Staff from 1940 onwards. A keen advocate of strategic bombing for most of the war – a policy which came to a chilling conclusion in the fire-bombing of Dresden.

- **Admiral Dudley Pound** (1877–1943) – Admiral of the Fleet and First Sea Lord from 1939. Fought the German U-boat threat until his until his death in 1943.
- **Admiral Andrew Cunningham** (1883–1963) – Became Admiral of the Fleet and First Sea Lord in October 1943 following the death of Pound.

At Sea – Biggest Battleships

Arguably one of the great follies of the war was the investment, by all sides, in battleships. Though these mighty titans of the sea played a huge role in the propaganda war, their effect in combat was minimal and they soon found themselves overshadowed in naval importance by aircraft carriers. Manned by thousands of men and rippling with the kind of ordinance that could throw a shell 30 miles, most spent their time hiding from submarines and the increasing danger of attack from the air. The SMS *Bismarck* took part in only one operation lasting just 137 hours (the Battle of Denmark Strait) before being sunk. The flagship of the British fleet, HMS *Hood*, was split in two in the same engagement. The largest of the all the battleships, the Imperial Japanese navy's INS *Yamato*, was deployed more widely. It fought in the Battles of Midway, Philippine Sea and Leyte Gulf, but sank only one other vessel before being destroyed.

The lack of success of these giants in conventional naval engagements, and the potential for huge losses in morale at home when they were sunk, meant that their duties were largely restricted to coastal bombardment by the end of the war. Below is our list of the biggest battleships:

INS *Yamato*, Japan	72,809 tons, 862ft
INS *Musashi*, Japan	72,809 tons, 862ft
USS *Iowa*, United States (BB-61)	55,710 tons, 887ft
USS *New Jersey*, United States (BB-62)	55,710 tons, 887ft
USS *Missouri*, United States (BB-63)	55,710 tons, 887ft
USS *Wisconsin*, United States (BB-64)	55,710 tons, 887ft
SMS *Bismarck*, Germany	50,153 tons, 823ft
SMS *Tirpitz*, Germany	50,153 tons, 823ft
Richelieu, France	47,500 tons, 812ft
Jean Bart, France	47,500 tons, 812ft
HMS *Hood*, Great Britain	46,200 tons, 860ft

Wartime Heroes – Escape Attempts from Colditz

Oflag IV-C, better known as Colditz, was a German *Sonderlager* (high-security prison camp) for officers, located in a castle which sat on top of steep cliffs above the town of Colditz in Saxony. The extreme location of the camp, and the fact it was the only facility of its kind within Germany, led Field Marshal Hermann Goering to foolishly declare it to be 'escape-proof'. This statement was like red rag to bull to its Allied inmates, many of whom had been transferred to Colditz specifically because of their multiple escapes from other prisoner of war camps.

Depending on whose account you read, between thirty and thirty-six British, Canadian, French, Polish, Dutch and Belgian officers successfully escaped from Colditz, and its name became inextricably linked to these and many other audacious but unsuccessful attempts. The imagination of the world was also captured by the sheer ingenuity of the prisoners, who fashioned tools from everyday items and uniforms from curtains, and hid money, radios and weapons in the most extraordinary places.

It is worth noting that escaping from the castle itself was only half the battle for these plucky POWs. Even when outside its walls they still had to travel hundreds of miles through enemy territory to reach safety. Below are a few of the attempts that didn't make it, and a list of those who did:

 The Canteen Tunnel

Using a manhole cover on the floor of the canteen, British prisoners gained access to the sewerage and drain system underneath the castle. Using crudely fashioned tools, they managed to extend the drain to create an exit on a small grassy area outside the castle's walls. The only drawback was that the area was overlooked and they would be easily visible to the duty sentry. The escape team somehow managed to collect a 500-Reichsmark bribe – a small fortune – for the guard they knew would be on duty. Despite paying 100 Reichsmarks up-front, the guard betrayed them and the commandant and his men were waiting. The guard in question kept the money, got extra leave and was awarded the War Service Cross for his duplicity.

The Packing Case

When a new commandant instigated rules restricting prisoners' personal belongings, POWs were instructed to put much of their gear into storage. Diminutive Flight Lieutenant Dominic Bruce immediately seized his chance and had his comrades seal him inside a 3ft-square Red Cross packing case, with just a file and a 40ft rope made of bed sheets. He made his escape later that night, but not before writing '*Die Luft in Colditz gefällt mir nicht mehr. Auf Wiedersehen!*' (The air in Colditz no longer agrees with me. Goodbye!) on the box. He was recaptured a week later attempting to stow away on a ship in Danzig.

The Clock Tower Tunnel

Between 1940 and 1942, nine French officers organised a tunnel-digging project, which began in the chapel's disused clock tower and descended into the ground through the shaft that previously contained the clock's ropes and weights. The Germans discovered the initial excavations and bricked shut the entrance to the clock tower, a move which, ironically, meant that digging could begin in earnest. Each night the sound of their efforts reverberated round the castle, which meant that while the German guards were unaware of the location of the new tunnel they were fully aware that tunnelling was going on. Over eight months, the French dug a tunnel that was 144ft long and 28ft deep using homemade tools constructed from kitchen utensils. In a cruel twist of fate, the entrance to the tunnel was finally discovered when the French men were just 6.5ft from their destination. The tunnel had cut thorough the stone foundations and thick wooden floor beams of the castle so, pragmatic to the end, their German captors presented the diggers with the bill for the damage they had caused to the building – some 12,000 Reichsmarks.

The Epic Rappel

Picking the locks of their cells to escape after getting themselves thrown into solitary confinement, Polish lieutenants Miki Surmanowicz and Mietek Chmiel made their bid by lowering themselves down the outer wall of the castle with a rope constructed from bed sheets. The escape was made all the more daring by the fact that the pair could only access the outer wall by climbing across the roof of the guard house. They were caught when the German guards heard the hobnailed boots of the escapees scraping down the outside of the guard house wall.

The French Officer

A French officer attempted to walk straight through the front gates of the castle dressed in his homemade disguise: as an intimidating and rather proper looking woman. Amazingly, he made it past the sentries but ran out of luck when his watch slipped off his wrist. A group of British prisoners who were exercising in the yard politely picked it up and called out to the 'woman'. When the French officer kept walking it was enough to alert the guards and the deception was discovered.

The Mattress

British officer 'Peter' Allan had himself sewn inside an old straw mattress when he noticed that the Germans were moving some bedding stock from the castle. The opportunist nature of the escape meant that he had little time to prepare, bar grabbing a single 50 Reichsmark note and a homemade Hitlerjugend outfit.

The mattress containing Allan was driven from the castle and unloaded into a shed nearby, where he cut himself free. As a fluent German speaker, Allan spent nine days on the run, hitch-hiking to Vienna – during which time he shared a car with two SS officers – before he was picked up in a park, exhausted and hungry, and returned to Colditz.

 The Colditz Glider

In one of the most ambitious escape attempts from Colditz, British pilots Jack Best and Bill Goldfinch built a full-size glider. The two-man glider was assembled by Goldfinch and Best in the lower attic of the chapel, which was largely obscured from the view of the Germans. The prisoners built a false wall to hide the workshop and slowly built the glider out of common items taken from around the castle. Its hundreds of ribs were constructed from bed slats, wing spars were fashioned from floor boards and tables, control wires were made from electrical wiring, while prison sleeping bags were used to skin it. The pair had planned to launch the glider using a pulley system powered by a falling metal bathtub full of concrete. Ultimately, the glider was never finished as the US army liberated the camp on 16 April 1945.

And the Ones that Got Away ...

 French Lieutenant Alain Le Ray – Escaped 11 April 1941 by hiding in a terraced house during a game of football then making his way to Switzerland.

 French Lieutenant René Collin – Escaped 31 May 1941 by climbing into the rafters of a pavilion during exercise. He made it back to France.

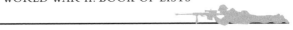

French Lieutenant Pierre Mairesse Lebrun – Escaped 2 July 1941 by vaulting over a wire in the park with the help of an associate. He reached Switzerland in eight days on a stolen bicycle.

Dutch Lieutenants Francis Steinmetz and E. Hans Larive – Escaped 15 August 1941 by hiding under a manhole cover during exercise. They took a train to Gottmadingen and reached Switzerland in three days.

Dutch Major C. Giebel and Dutch Lieutenant O.L. Drijber – Escaped 20 September 1941 by hiding under the same manhole cover as Steinmetz.

British Lieutenant Airey M.S. Neave and Dutch Lieutenant Anthony Luteyn – Escaped 5 January 1942 by crawling through a hole in a camp theatre and walking out dressed as German soldiers. They reached Switzerland two days later.

British Lieutenant H.N. Fowler and Dutch Lieutenant Damiaen Joan van Doorninck – Escaped 9 September 1942 by dressing as a German officer and a Polish orderly. They managed to reach Switzerland.

British Captain Patrick R. Reid, British Major Ronald B. Littledale, British Lieutenant-Commander William E. Stephens and Canadian Flight Lieutenant Howard D. Wardle – Escaped 14 October 1942 by slipping through the POW kitchens and into the German yard. They took five days to reach Switzerland.

Ten Technological Advances of the War

/ Jet Fighters

The Me 262 Schwalbe ('Swallow') was the first jet fighter to see combat. With a top speed of over 550mph, it was faster than any other aircraft in the war and claimed over 500 Allied kills. The Gloster Meteor, a British-manufactured turbojet fighter, was the only Allied jet fighter to enter combat.

/ Assault Rifles

The German FG42 is widely accepted as the most advanced machine gun of the Second World War. Developed specifically for the use by Fallschirmjäger airborne infantry, this multi-purpose weapon combined the firepower of a light machine gun with the portability of a standard issue rifle. Though it was only produced in small numbers, this weapon, along with the StG 44 semi-automatic rifle, served as the template for the modern assault rifles used today.

/ Cruise Missiles

Arguably the Fieseler Fi 103 (better known as the V-1 rocket, or the 'Doodlebug') was the world's first cruise missile. Once it had been pointed in the right direction, this pulse-jet-powered rocket used a simple autopilot controlled by a nose-mounted gyroscope to regulate its height and speed. A basic odometer driven by a vane anemometer counted down the distance to its target area, literally dropping the lethal payload out of the sky when the pre-set distance had been reached. The V-1 could deliver its payload over 40 miles; easily reaching London from occupied northern France. More than 8,000 were launched in the early years of the war, claiming some 20,000 casualties.

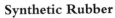

Synthetic Rubber

From truck tyres to gun sights, rubber was used in almost every mechanised machine of the war. Since most of the world's supply of natural rubber was found in Axis territory by mid-1942, the production of synthetic rubber in the United States became essential to the war effort. By 1944, a total of fifty factories in the US were manufacturing it, pouring out twice the volume of the world's natural rubber production before the beginning of the war.

RADAR

RADAR (short for 'radio detection and ranging') used bounced electromagnetic waves to pinpoint the range, altitude, direction and speed of moving objects, such as planes, ships and vehicles. The British were the first to fully deploy RADAR as a defence against aircraft attack. By 1940 the RAF had set up a chain network of RADAR beacons along the south coast of England. The new technology allowed Fighter Command to accurately identify the position of incoming Luftwaffe aircraft; an advantage which proved crucial in the RAF's victory during the Battle of Britain.

Penicillin

Though first discovered in 1928, penicillin was not developed to a degree where it could be safely mass-produced until halfway through the war. In 1943 the War Production Board in the US ordered the wide-scale distribution of penicillin to Allied troops in Europe. By the time of the assault on Normandy in 1944, some 2.3 million doses were carried into battle. The drug made a major difference in the number of deaths and amputations caused by infected wounds among Allied forces, saving thousands of lives.

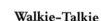

Walkie-Talkie

The first hand-held, portable, two-way radio transceiver was developed during the war by Motorola, allowing small infantry units on the ground to co-ordinate their movements easily. The term 'walkie-talkie' referred to the Motorola SCR-300 held in a backpack with a detachable handset. Motorola also produced a one piece hand-held unit, the AM SCR-536 radio ('handie-talkie' (HT)). Both devices ran on vacuum tubes and used high-voltage dry cell batteries.

Heated Flying Suits

Electrically heated suits were introduced by Lion Apparel in conjunction with General Electric during the war. They soon proved to be a huge advance on the bulky leather and sheepskin clothing previously worn by airmen. The battery-powered suits were used by patrol and bomber crews who flew for long periods in the cold air above 30,000ft, and especially by the waist gunners who fired through open window gun ports. However, by the end of the war heated and pressurised cabins would render them obsolete.

Plasma

Dried plasma was developed in the war as a blood substitute. The isolation of this fluid, which could be easily transported and stored, was vital to life. It allowed medics to help those who had lost blood; supplying minerals and administering fluids to injured soldiers. A dried plasma package for the armed forces came in two tin cans, each containing 400cc bottles (one bottle contained dried plasma, the other enough distilled water to reconstitute it). By the end of the war the Red Cross Blood Bank in New York had provided enough blood for over 6 million plasma packages.

Spam

Widely issued to Allied troops in the war – especially where fresh meat was difficult to get – and served in an unappealing aluminium tin, this pre-cooked meat product was first produced by the Hormel Foods Corporation in 1937. Spam was usually made from chopped pork shoulder meat. Salt, water and potato starch was then added and the results set in aspic. Despite its ubiquitous nature, Spam was never that popular with the GIs and was often referred to as 'ham that didn't pass its physical', or 'meatloaf without basic training'.

The Cost of War – Hitler's Plans for Great Britain

'Since England, in spite of her hopeless military situation, shows no signs of being ready to come to a compromise, I have decided to prepare a landing operation against England, and if necessary to carry it out.' With these words Hitler began preparations for Operation Sea Lion – the invasion of Great Britain by Nazi forces.

Had Operation Sea Lion been a success, Britain would have become a very different place. According to detailed plans created for the post-invasion administration:

- Britain and Ireland were to be divided into six military-economic commands, with headquarters in London, Birmingham, Newcastle, Liverpool, Glasgow and Dublin.

- Whiteleys shopping centre in Bayswater was to be the initial headquarters of the Wehrmacht in London, but Hitler ultimately had his eye on the ancestral home of Winston Churchill, Blenheim Palace, as the nerve centre of the German occupation.

- As in Norway, a puppet government was to be put in place. It has been claimed that the abdicated king, Edward VIII, was offered the throne in the event of a German invasion, but this has not been substantiated.

- The OKW (*Oberkommando der Wehrmacht* – high command of the Third Reich armed forces), RSHA (*Reichssicherheitshauptamt* – Reich Main Security Office) and Foreign Ministry all compiled lists of those they thought could form a new civil government. The list was headed by British aristocrat and founder of the British Union of Fascists Oswald Mosley.

- Einsatzgruppen under Dr Franz Six were to follow the invasion force to establish the New Nazi Order. They were provided with a list (known as The Black Book) of 2,820 people to be arrested immediately.

- The Einsatzgruppen were tasked with liquidating what remained of Britain's Jewish population, which numbered over 300,000.

- Dr Six had also been entrusted with the task of pillaging anything of financial, military, industrial or cultural value, securing 'aero-technological research results and important equipment', as well as 'Germanic works of art'. There is also a suggestion that he toyed with the idea of moving Nelson's Column to Berlin.

- According to captured German documents, the commander-in-chief of the German army, Walther von Brauchitsch, had directed that 'The able-bodied male population between the ages of 17 and 45 will, unless the local situation calls for an exceptional ruling, be interned and dispatched to the Continent'. This most likely refers to the transportation of British men as industrial slave labour to factories and mines across the Reich.

Feeding the Nation – Ration Books

As German U-boats cut off supplies of food and other goods from abroad, rationing became a fact of life for the civilian population of Great Britain throughout the war. To put the success of the German stranglehold on British supply lines in perspective: before the war the country had imported some 55 million tons of food, by early 1940 this figure had dropped to 12 million, leaving the population close to starvation.

The ration book became a lifeline for most households in Britain, with every man, woman and child being issued with their own copy. While people still paid for their goods with money, the books contained coupons that shopkeepers cut out or signed to ensure everyone received their fair entitlement to food and other items. Each adult was allowed a specific amount of basic food items, typically this included:

	Meat	1–2s (5–10d) per head per week
	Bacon	4–8oz (113–227g) per week
	Tea	2–4oz (57–113g) per week
	Cheese	1–8oz (28–227g) per week
	Sugar	8oz (227g) per week
	Lard or butter	4oz (113g) per week

There were also different coloured ration books to ensure everyone got the right amount and types of food they needed for basic health:

- Buff ration books were issued to adults.
- Green ration books were issued to pregnant women, nursing mothers and children under 5 – to ensure they had first choice of fruit, a daily pint of milk and a double supply of eggs.
- Blue ration books were issued to children between 5 and 16 years of age – to ensure they had fruit, the full meat ration and half a pint of milk a day.

With everyone pulling together in the face of adversity, rationing was nothing if not egalitarian and, in a remarkably progressive concession for the time, vegetarians were even permitted to swap their meat coupons for other foods.

Blitzkrieg!

Blitzkrieg is a naturalised German word, literally meaning 'lightning war'. It was coined by western journalists observing the German progress though France in 1939 to describe a new form of armoured warfare practice by the Wehrmacht. Blitzkreig was a concentration of tanks, infantry, artillery and air power delivered to punch through enemy lines at high speed. Indeed, the sheer speed of German advances made it very difficult for their enemies to rally effectively at any given point, as the front had moved by the time they did so. When this was combined with systematic application of infiltration and the bypassing of traditional enemy strongpoints, whole nations toppled in a matter of months.

Arguably, the co-ordination of forces was not a new idea and such tactics of 'total war' had been used since the Napoleonic era, however the advances in technology meant that the constant movement and devastating firepower of the German troops was breathtakingly effective in the early years of the war. Below we track the course and the speed of the Nazi blitzkrieg:

 Poland – The invasion of Poland began on 1 September 1939, one week after the signing of the Molotov–Ribbentrop Pact, and ended on 8 October 1939 with the annexing of the western Poland.

 The Netherlands – In the Netherlands the battle lasted just four days, from 10 May 1940 until 14 May 1940, when the main Dutch forces surrendered.

 Belgium – The Germans invaded Belgium on 10 May 1940 and the Belgian army surrendered on 28 May 1940.

 France – France was invaded on 10 May 1940 and an armistice was signed between France and Germany just over a month later, on 25 June 1940.

🏺 **The Soviet Union** – The invasion of the Soviet Union was to expose the flaws in the blitzkrieg tactic. In the vast open spaces of the Russian steppes, such pace could not be maintained. Having not allowed enough time to reach Moscow before the Russian winter closed in, the bulk of the German invasion force found themselves overstretched and ill-equipped as they ground to a halt in the freezing conditions. Despite rallying the following spring, Hitler's armies would be bogged down in bitter fighting that would last for three brutal years.

Best War Video Games

With so many theatres of war, truly epic battles and a huge range of weapons to choose from, it is no surprise that video games set during the Second World War have been perennially popular with gamers. Second World War games have been produced in most gaming genres, from first-person shooters to flight simulators and real-time strategy games. While many early games sought to capture historical accuracy and recreate strategic challenges, more recently there has been a trend towards recreating the cinematic impact of Hollywood blockbusters such as *Saving Private Ryan* and *Band of Brothers*. Here are some of the best:

Call of Duty – The Call of Duty series is a first- and third-person shooter franchise, which began on the PC and soon expanded onto consoles and hand-helds. Primarily set in the Second World War, the series has featured campaigns from most of the major theatres of war and often aped classic movie set pieces. To date, the games have shifted over 50 million units worldwide. Fast-paced and brutal.

Medal of Honor – Arguably the game that kicked off the immersive first-person shooter genre in Second World War games, the Medal of Honor series was created by film-maker Steven Spielberg's DreamWorks movie studio. As a result, the early games were revolutionary in their atmospheric, cinematic tone. The games cast the player as an Allied soldier completing a series of suspenseful tasks, and contain fewer of the out-and-out assault scenes found in Call of Duty. Thrilling but slow-moving in parts.

Castle Wolfenstein 3D and Return to Castle Wolfenstein – The first edition of this classic 1991 game was a Doom clone that simply had players blasting their way out of dungeon overrun with evil Nazis. Later editions greatly improved their graphics and enhanced the storyline to cast the gamer as an Allied agent from the fictional Office of Secret Actions (OSA), sent to investigate the activities of Heinrich Himmler's SS Paranormal Division. Despite these developments, the action still takes place in eerie Castle Wolfenstein and you still have to blast your way through evil Nazis. Bloody hokum but great fun.

Battlefield 1942 – Battlefield 1942 is a history buff's dream. The game allows you to play the role of one of five classes of soldier, drive more than thirty-five vehicles and use authentic-looking and sounding weapons. Battlefield 1942 contains the best features from other first-person shooters, such as Medal of Honor and

Return to Castle Wolfenstein, and combines them with many features of its own that make it probably one of the best ever, all round Second World War gaming experiences. Enormous and eminently playable.

Commandos 1, 2 and 3 – This action-strategy game lets you take control of a group of quirky soldiers working behind enemy lines. With each character possessing a different skill and a series of challenging stealth-based missions to complete, the games provide a great blend of action and tension supported by excellent graphics. Funny and engrossing, but sometimes difficult to play.

Microsoft Combat Flight Simulator 2: Pacific Theatre – Probably the best of the Microsoft combat flight simulators, this game combines a state-of-the-art (for the time) flight package with open-ended architecture that allows its fans to create their own scenery, aircraft, missions and even the campaigns themselves. Nerdy but rewarding.

Silent Hunter 4 – This game places the player in command of an American submarine in the Pacific Theatre. The graphics for Silent Hunter 4 were improved massively from previous games and contribute to the Hollywood feel of the game play. Great if you've ever wanted to torpedo a battleship.

In the Army – Standard Combat Equipment for Wehrmacht Soldiers

Despite the German army's often fearsome reputation for discipline and devastating efficiency in the war, it was far from the motorised high-tech automation that contemporary propaganda would have led the public to believe. At the start of the war, the German army (*Heer*) only had a minority of its formations motorised; its infantry remained approximately 90 per cent foot-borne throughout the war, and much of its artillery still depended on horse-drawn transport. As the war went on, shortages in materials and disruption of supply lines meant that, more often than not, German infantrymen depended on the kit they could carry with them. Below is selection of what the average German soldier took into the field:

- **Steel Helmet** (*Stahlhelm*) – The classic German steel helmet was modified from the original 1935 design in 1940 and in 1942, in both cases to make it cheaper to produce. The helmet was held in place with a leather chin strap, and often adapted by individual soldiers with various camouflage paint schemes and covers.
- **Belt** (*Koppel*) – The average soldier wore a smooth leather 4.4cm-wide belt. A webbing belt was introduced in Africa and later on the Continent, starting in 1943. Material shortages late in the war resulted in an artificial leather (*Press-stoff*) version.
- **Buckle** (*Koppelschloss*) – The standard buckle was adopted in 1936, replacing the *Reichswehr* version. They were made of stamped aluminium or steel, and, although they were painted various colours, all featured the German eagle and the phrase '*GOTT MIT UNS*' (God is with us).
- **Y-Straps** (*Tragneriemen*) – Y-straps were used to support the weight of personal equipment and ammunition. They featured

three leather straps: two in the front that attached to ammunition pouch D-rings and a single strap that attached to the belt at the back. The three straps were connected to each other between the shoulder blades with a steel O-ring. Two additional straps were fixed in the front and extended beneath the arms to support a pack or rucksack.

Bread Bag (*Brotbeutel*) – The bread bag had been a traditional piece of field equipment for German soldiers since the early 1800s. Used by soldiers to carry a bread ration, it was a simple canvas bag with two straps and a hook to attach to a belt. The outer surface contained loops to attach a canteen and mess kit.

Canteen (*Feldflasche*) – The M1931 field canteen was an unpainted aluminium or enabled steel 0.8L flask, sometimes fitted with an insulating felt cover to aid concealment and to preserve the contents.

Ammunition Pouches (*Patronentasche*) – The M1911 leather ammo pouch had three pockets holding two 5-round clips of 7.92mm ammunition, 30 rounds per pouch.

Entrenching Tool (*Kleines Schannzzeug*) – Mostly unchanged since its adoption in the 1880s, this small spade had a square steel blade and a short wooden handle. The blade was painted black but the handle was left with a natural finish to prevent blisters.

Bayonet (*Seitengewehr*) – The K98k bayonet's official name is 'Seitengewehr (SG) 84/98'. Early versions were made with wooden hand grips, but wartime production restrictions meant brown Bakelite grips became more common. The bayonet could be attached to the end of the Mauser K98k.

Gas Mask (*Gasmaske*) – The M1930 and M1938 gas mask was stored in a fluted steel canister slung over the shoulder with green webbing. The gas mask may also have had a Gas Cape Pouch (*Gasplane*) attached at the top.

Wartime Heroes – Most Decorated Soldiers

Audie Leon Murphy (20 June 1924–28 May 1971)
Murphy was the most decorated American soldier of the Second World War. He served for twenty-seven months in action in the European Theatre, during which time he received the Medal of Honor (for a single-handed battle with a squad of German soldiers while wounded), the Distinguished Service Cross (for destroying a machine-gun nest that had just killed his friend) and thirty-one other US and foreign medals and citations (including five from France and one from Belgium). After the war he became a movie star and country singer, whose films included *To Hell and Back,* which was based on his autobiography. He died in a plane crash in 1971 and was interred, with full military honours, in Arlington National Cemetery.

Hans-Ulrich Rudel (2 July 1916–18 December 1982)
Rudel was a Stuka dive bomber pilot and a member of the Nazi Party who became the most highly decorated German serviceman of the war. Rudel flew more that 2,530 combat missions and destroyed a total of 2,000 targets; including 800 vehicles, 519 tanks, 150 artillery pieces, 70 landing craft, 4 armoured trains, 2 cruisers, 1 destroyer, 1 Soviet battleship and several bridges. He lost

his leg below the knee in the process and ended the war in an America hospital. Rudel was awarded the Wound Badge in Gold, the German Cross in Gold, the Pilot's and Observer's Badge with Diamonds, and the Front Flying Clasp of the Luftwaffe with 2,000 sorties in Diamonds. He was the only recipient of the Knight's Cross of the Iron Cross with Golden Oak Leaves, Swords and Diamonds. Indeed, the only man more honoured by the Luftwaffe was Hermann Goering himself. After the hostilities ceased he initially moved to Argentina, before returning to West Germany in 1953 to become a successful businessman and a leading figure in German politics.

8 Lieutenant-Colonel Robert Blair 'Paddy' Mayne (1915–55)

Mayne was probably the most decorated British soldier of the Second World War. After volunteering to join the newly formed No. 11 Commando in 1940, Mayne saw action in North Africa, Scandinavia and Europe, and contributed to founding the SAS along the way. Mayne pioneered the use of armoured jeeps to conduct surprise attacks on enemy airfields, and is said to have personally destroyed 130 aircraft using this technique. He received the Distinguished Service Order with three bars (one of only seven British servicemen to do so), 1939–45 Star, Africa Star and 8th Army Bar, Italy Star, France and Germany Star, Defence Medal, War Medal and Oak Leaf. In addition to this he also received the Legion d'Honneur and the Croix de Guerre for his work with the French Resistance. It has often been questioned why Mayne was not awarded the Victoria Cross. Mayne, who had been a rugby international before war, worked in polar exploration when hostilities ended before settling down as a solicitor. Tragically, he died in a car accident in 1955.

Marshal of the Soviet Union Georgy Konstantinovich Zhukov (1896–1974)

Zhukov was a career solider in the Red Army who became the most decorated general in the history of the Soviet Union. During the Second World War he played a key role in the defence and liberation of the Soviet Union following the German invasion in 1941, and led the fight to capture Berlin. The list of his honours is too long to recount in full, but he achieved the Order of Victory (twice), Gold Star of Hero of the Soviet Union (four times), Order of Lenin (six times), Order of the October Revolution, Order of the Red Banner (three times), Order of Suvorov 1st class (twice) and the Marshal's Star. Despite being born a peasant, Zhukov became a politician after the war. He served as Minister of Defence under Nikita Khrushchev and was instrumental in the invasion of Hungary. Zhukov continued to support the interests of the military over those of his political masters, however, and was eventually forced into early retirement.

Entertaining the Troops – ENSA Goes to War

 The Entertainments National Service Association, or ENSA, was an organisation set up in 1939 by Basil Dean and Leslie Henson to provide off-duty recreation for British armed forces.

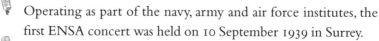

- Operating as part of the navy, army and air force institutes, the first ENSA concert was held on 10 September 1939 in Surrey.
- ENSA put companies of professional and amateur performers into almost every theatre of war to supply upbeat, moral-boosting variety shows filled with popular songs, as well as more hokey fare like contortionists, magicians and impressionists.
- ENSA was a much appreciated diversion from the horrors of war, but the geographical ambition of the programme meant that, inevitably, some of its acts were far from professional. Before long it earned the affectionate yet mocking nickname among the troops of 'Every Night Something Awful'.
- By the standards of the time, ENSA paid well in an effort to secure quality performers: £10 a week went to featured acts and a respectable £4 a week to those in the chorus.
- Many famous stars of the time performed for them including Arthur Askey, Gracie Fields, Vera Lynn, George Formby, Tommy Cooper and Joyce Grenfell. Even the likes of Sir Laurence Olivier and Sir Ralph Richardson did their bit when they donned the uniform of honorary lieutenants and undertook a six-week tour of Europe performing plays by Shakespeare.
- Despite their regular performances close to the front line, only one member of ENSA lost their life in the field. Vivienne Fayre was killed whilst travelling on an ENSA bus in France on 23 January 1945.
- The last ENSA performance took place in India on 18 August 1946. After the war, ENSA was superseded by Combined Services Entertainment (CSE), which now operates as part of the Services Sound and Vision Corporation (SSVC).

At Sea – Japan's Surprise Attack on Pearl Harbor

The surprise attack by Imperial Japanese forces on American bases in Pearl Harbor on 7 December 1941 caught the United States Pacific Fleet completely unprepared, and brought this formerly neutral giant into the war. Below are some statistics relating to the attack:

- The Japanese launched a three-wave attack on the harbour, which consisted of 5 midget submarines and some 360 planes.
- Anchored in Pearl Harbor were 93 vessels, including 8 battleships, as well as army forces including the 24th and 25th Infantry Divisions. A total of 390 navy and army planes of various types were present on the airfields surrounding the base.
- All together the Japanese sank or severely damaged 18 ships, including the 8 battleships, 3 light cruisers and 3 destroyers. On the airfields the Japanese destroyed 161 US planes (army 74, navy 87), and seriously damaged 102 (army 71, navy 31).
- The navy and marine corps suffered a total of 2,896 casualties, of which 2,117 were deaths (navy 2,008, marines 109), and 779 wounded (navy 710, marines 69). The army suffered 228 killed and 113 seriously wounded. In addition, at least 57 civilians were killed.
- Despite the perception of this battle as a devastating blow to America, only three of the ships hit were permanently lost to the US navy. These were the battleships USS *Arizona*, USS *Oklahoma* and the old battleship USS *Utah* (then used as a target ship).
- Four of the ships sunk during the attack were later raised and returned to duty, including the battleships USS *California*, USS *West Virginia* and USS *Nevada*. Even those ships that were so damaged they needed to be scrapped were stripped of usable material, including gun turrets and ordinance.

Perhaps the greatest legacy of the assault in real terms was the national trauma of a sudden attack on home soil. This was something that the United States took many years to recover from.

Five Wartime Spies

Virginia Hall

Know to the German Gestapo as 'Artemis', Virginia Hall went by many names, including 'Germaine', 'Camille', 'Diane', and 'Marie Monin'. As a young woman, Hall had studied and travelled extensively in Europe. Early in her career she lost her leg in a hunting accident, but this failed to slow her down and by the fall of France she was working in the ambulance service. She promptly joined Special Operations Executive (SOE) and operated in Vichy France co-ordinating the underground resistance movements. When the Germans occupied southern France in 1942, Hall escaped through Spain only to return later that year to work under the code name 'Diane' for the American Office of Strategic Services (OSS). Here she mapped drop zones to facilitate the delivery of supplies from England, sourced safe houses and even linked up with a Jedburgh Team (a group of guerrilla fighters parachuted behind enemy lines ahead of the

main invasion) to provide help on the ground as the Allied forces landed at Normandy.

Klaus Fuchs

Fuchs was a German-born physicist who first became involved with the Communist Party while studying in Germany. Fleeing the Nazi government, he moved to England where he worked on the British atomic bomb project and began to supply information to the Soviets. In 1943 he was transferred to the US to assist on the Manhattan project where, for two years, he continued to pass information to the KGB about the plans for the bomb and the production of uranium 235. On his return to England in 1946 he was captured when details of his activities were exposed in decoded Soviet transmissions. He was tried and sentenced to fourteen years' imprisonment.

Ian Fleming

Codenamed 17F, the creator of James Bond was recruited by Rear Admiral John Henry Godfrey, Director of Naval Intelligence for the Royal Navy, in 1939. During his time in naval intelligence, Fleming instigated several daring plans. Operation Ruthless proposed to crash a captured German aircraft into the English Channel so that a British crew, dressed in Luftwaffe uniforms, could hijack German patrol boats and capture an Engima machine. Operation Mincemeat attached false documents to a corpse which was deliberately allowed to wash up on a beach in Punta Umbría in Spain to deceive the Germans about Allied plans for the invasion of Sicily. Later in the war, Fleming would direct operations for two tactical commando assault teams: 30 Assault Unit and T force.

Princess Noor-un-nisa Inayat Khan

Formerly a children's author, at the outbreak of war the princess enrolled in SOE where she was trained as a wireless operator and sent into occupied France. Serving as the sole communications link between her unit of the French Resistance and their British base, the princess eluded the Gestapo for months by cycling from one safe house to another with her transmitter hidden in the basket of her bicycle. She was, however, eventually captured by the Germans and executed.

Wing Commander Edward Yeo-Thomas

Codenamed 'The White Rabbit', Forest Frederic Edward Yeo-Thomas spent most of the war behind enemy lines. Yeo-Thomas grew up in France but was educated in England and had served in the army in the First World War. He joined the RAF when the Second World War broke out, but after serving for two years as an intelligence officer he decided he wanted a more active part in the hostilities and joined SOE in 1942. He parachuted into France, where he organised the dropping of supplies and co-ordinated planning with underground group leaders. Despite evading capture multiple times (in one instance by hiding in a hearse), he was ultimately captured by the Gestapo and tortured before being sent to the notorious Buchenwald concentration camp until the end of the war.

Top Operations – The Race for 'Heavy Water'

The devastation wreaked on the Japanese cities of Nagasaki and Hiroshima by a single weapon was an emphatic sign of just how pivotal the race to develop a nuclear bomb was in the war. Though the Allies eventually won this deadly competition, between 1940 and 1943 they waged a secret battle to stop Germany conducting research into a similar super-weapon.

Ironically, the nuclear-fission process required to create such a device could be achieved fairly easily by scientists on both sides by bombarding uranium or plutonium with neutrons. It was finding a stable method to control subsequent chain reactions which eluded them. One potential solution was the use of deuterium oxide, or 'heavy water'. Unfortunately for the Allies, the pre-wartime centre of the production of this was the Vemork Hydroelectric Plant in Norway, which had fallen under German control following their invasion of Norway in 1940. Though the Deuxième Bureau (French military intelligence) had removed 185kg of heavy water from the plant prior to its capture by the Germans, the installation itself still remained capable of producing it.

Between 1940 and 1944 a series of daring sabotage actions, co-ordinated with the Norwegian Resistance, resulted in the destruction of the plant and all the heavy water it had produced:

Operation Grouse – In 1942 the British Special Operations Executive (SOE) successfully placed four Norwegian nationals as an advance team on the Hardanger Plateau, above the plant, to observe the daily routines of its staff and gather intelligence.

Operation Freshman – Later in 1942, British paratroopers mounted an aerial assault against the plant using gliders.

They failed to rendezvous with the spotters of Operation Grouse, however, and almost all the participants were either killed when their planes crashed in harsh weather or were captured by the Gestapo.

Operation Gunnerside – In 1943 SOE mounted another attack, in which a team of trained Norwegian commandos managed to infiltrate the production facility and halt production by destroying vital electrolysis chambers with explosives.

Allied Bombing – When Operation Gunnerside did not destroy the plant itself, it was followed up with heavy bombing. Exhausted by the assaults, the Germans ceased operations and attempted to move the remaining heavy water to Germany.

Norwegian Resistance – Norwegian resistance forces then completed their mission by sinking the SF *Hydro,* the ferry transporting the invaluable cargo, as it crossed Lake Tinnsjø; effectively ending the Nazi nuclear programme.

Blitz!

The Blitz is the name commonly given to the sustained bombing of the British mainland by the German Luftwaffe, between 7 September 1940 and 10 May 1941.

In popular memory the Blitz was largely associated with London, but it actually affected industrial and military cities right across the UK; including Aberdeen, Belfast, Birmingham, Brighton, Bristol, Cardiff, Coventry, Eastbourne, Exeter, Glasgow, Liverpool, Manchester, Nottingham, Plymouth, Portsmouth, Sheffield, Southampton, Sunderland and Swansea. Hundreds of individual bombs were also dropped across the country as returning aircraft dumped unused ordinance.

The Blitz can largely be divided into three phases:

- The first began on 7 September 1940 with the bombing of London on consecutive nights. During this period more than 1 million houses were destroyed or damaged.
- The second ran from November 1940 to February 1941. This saw the Luftwaffe widen the focus of its attacks to include industrial cities and ports, notably the home of the Spitfire, Coventry, which saw its city centre and famous cathedral all but destroyed.
- The third ran between February and May 1941, in which the Luftwaffe concentrated its efforts against ports and ship-building facilities in an effort to weaken British sea power.

The single most devastating raid of the Blitz occurred on 29 December 1940, when German aircraft attacked London at night with incendiaries and high-explosive bombs. The aerial assault caused a savage firestorm that has since been called the Second Great Fire of London. As the nation's capital bore the brunt of the assault, its residents sheltered in Underground stations and home-constructed shelters. Among the many significant buildings which were destroyed or heavily damaged were: Arsenal Football Stadium, Chelsea Old Church, the Balham and Euston Tube Stations, Lambeth Walk and the Great Synagogue of London.

As an attempt to soften the country up before a full invasion, the Blitz was a failure. By wasting time and resources bombing civilians, the Luftwaffe allowed a depleted RAF to regroup – a mistake which ultimately led to the Germans' defeat during the Battle of Britain. More chillingly, Allied forces now had no qualms about undertaking similar civilian-focussed bombing campaigns against their enemy, and German cities would reap the whirlwind of their actions.

Death From Above – Top Ten Bombers

 Heinkel 111

Though its unique 'greenhouse' cockpit made the Heinkel 111 one of the most recognisable bombers of the war, it had a background in deception. Often described as a wolf in sheep's clothing, it masqueraded as a transport aircraft before the war – when Germany was still forbidden to produce armaments as a result of restrictions levied by the Treaty of Versailles – but its true purpose was to provide the Luftwaffe with a medium bomber. The Heinkel 111 was used extensively in the European Theatre at the start of the war, but its lack of speed and defensive armament rendered it obsolete toward the end of hostilities.

Aichi D3A

The first Japanese plane to bomb American targets in the war and the plane that sank more Allied shipping than any other, the Aichi D3A, known as 'Val' to Allied forces, was one of the best dive bombers of its time. Easy to recognise due to its fixed landing gear and unique elliptical wing design, the D3A had a two-man crew and carried a single 250kg bomb. In the latter half of the war their vulnerability to Allied fighters rendered the aircraft obsolete, and most of the remaining Vals were used in kamikaze attacks.

De Havilland Mosquito

Nicknamed 'The Wooden Wonder' as a nod to its wooden frame and balsa wood panelling, the Mosquito was a long-range medium bomber known for its impressive speed, which carried a single 1.8 ton bomb. The Mosquito saw action in Europe and the Pacific where, as it was largely unarmed, the aircraft relied on its speed and agility for self-defence. Despite the fact that its loss rate was lowest of all Allied bombers, and its bombing precision rating the highest, the RAF failed to utilise the Mosquito's potential and relegated the aircraft to night fighter and bomber support roles.

Junkers 87 Stuka

A key airborne element of the terrifying onslaught of the Nazi blitzkrieg attack, the Stuka was a single-engine precision dive bomber carrying a crew of two and a single 1.8 ton bomb. Commonly used for tactical support throughout the war, the plane became famous for its *Jericho-Trompete* ('Jericho Trumpet'), a wailing siren housed in the plane's nose, which terrified men on the ground and become synonymous with German air power in the early years of the war.

Avro Lancaster

The Lancaster secured its place in popular culture by delivering Barnes Wallis' bouncing bomb against German dams in the Ruhr Valley during Operation Chastise. But this four-engine, long-range night bomber was also the main British heavy bomber used during the second half of the war. It flew over 150,000 sorties and had a range that could cover all of Germany. The aircraft could carry up to 10 tons of bombs and defended itself with three turrets and eight machine guns.

B-17 Flying Fortress

The world's first four-engine, long-range heavy bomber (launched in 1935), the Flying Fortress was so called as it was designed to protect itself rather than rely on fighter support. It did this by covering all angles of potential attack with eight gun positions, placed strategically around the aircraft, supporting thirteen heavy machine guns. The brilliance of its basic design would enable the production of ever-improved versions of the aircraft, and it fought in every major theatre until the end of the war. Equipped with advanced electronics for its time, the Flying Fortress had a crew of ten and could carry over 5 tons of bombs.

B-24 Liberator

First deployed in 1941, the Liberator was a four-engine heavy bomber which boasted the longest range of any Allied aircraft (over 2,000 miles). It was also the most produced American military aircraft, with 18,400 units being shipped. The Liberator carried up to 6 tons of bombs and struck as far into Nazi-occupied territory as the Ploesti oil fields in Romania. It was also commonly used in long-range anti-submarine patrols all over the Atlantic Ocean.

B-29 Superfortress

This huge four-engine, long-range heavy bomber could carry up to 9 tons of bombs internally, and a further two 10-ton bombs under its wings. The design and electronics used meant it was extremely advanced for its time, and the plane included such features such as a pressurised cabin, an electronic fire-control system and remote-controlled machine-gun turrets. Initially deployed in high-altitude day missions in the Pacific Theatre, towards the end of the war the Superfortress was stripped of its weaponry to fly stealthy night missions at low altitude, where it mercilessly destroyed Japan's cities with incendiary bombs. Indeed, the Superfortess secured its ominous position as a weapon of mass destruction when it ended the war by dropping the atomic bomb on Hiroshima and Nagasaki.

 Junkers Ju-88

Carrying up to 3 tons of bombs, this supremely versatile twin-engine, medium-range bomber was used by the Luftwaffe throughout the war. Affectionately known as the 'The Maid of all Work', the Ju-88 was inventively modified throughout the conflict to play a range of roles – a fighter bomber, a night fighter and even a dive bomber – throughout its illustrious career.

 Mitsubishi G4M3

Nicknamed the 'Flying Cigar' because of its unique shape and the fact that its unprotected fuel tanks easily caught fire, the Mitsubishi G4M was the most ubiquitous Japanese bomber of the war. Designed as a land-based bomber where a high speed and excellent range (over 2,600 miles) were the chief requirements, the G4M achieved these by an almost complete disregard for armour and the protection of those onboard. The aircraft's seven-man crew could carry bombs or torpedoes, but were soon found to be horribly vulnerable to attack.

Wartime Lingo – British Regimental Mottos

A regimental motto is a motivational phrase which sums up the attitude of a given regiment. These may have been created along with the regiment itself – like the adoption of '*Nulli Secundus*' (Second to None) by the Coldstream Guards when they were placed as the second senior regiment of the Household Troops – or ascribed to a regiment after a famous victory – like '*Faugh a ballagh*' (Clear the way), which was adopted by the Royal Irish Rangers in the Peninsular War when English troops under Wellington failed to breach the gates of the Badajoz and the regiment was brought in to finish the job. Though a motto may be written in any language, Latin and French are the most commonly used. Here are ten of the most well known:

- '*Quis Separabit*' (Who Shall Separate Us) – Irish Guards
- '*Utrinque paratus*' (Ready for anything) – The Parachute Regiment
- '*Ubique! Quo fas et gloria ducunt*' (Everywhere! Where right and glory lead) – The Royal Regiment of Artillery
- '*Nec aspera terrent*' (Difficulties be damned) – King's Regiment, King's Liverpool Regiment

- *'Per Mare, Per Terram'* (By Sea, By Land) – Royal Marines
- *'Cede nullis'* (Yield to none) – The King's Own Yorkshire Light Infantry
- *'Nemo me impune lacessit'* (None attack me with impunity) – Scots Guards, Royal Scots, Black Watch, 42nd Highlanders
- *'Pristinae virtutis memores'* (Mindful of former valour) – 8th King's Royal Irish Hussars
- *'Honi soit qui mal y pense'* (Evil be to him who evil thinks) – Household Cavalry
- *'Sans Peur'* (Without Fear) – Argyll & Sutherland Highlanders

The Cost of War – Soviet Snipers in Stalingrad

The Battle of Stalingrad saw the might of the German assault on the Soviet Union grind to a halt. Despite the fact that the Germans managed to occupy some 90 per cent of the city, the resilience of the Soviets and their willingness to pour reinforcements – often without weapons – into the war zone meant the battle soon broke down into bitter street fighting. More familiar with lightning-fast moving assaults, well-supported by amour and air power, the Germans called it *Rattenkreig* – Rat War.

During eight terrible months, between 23 August 1942 and 2 February 1943, both sides indiscriminately bombed and shelled what was left of the streets and buildings, turning the city into ruins. Within this hellish environment, the Soviets developed a new military tactic of deploying snipers to demoralise enemy troops. Soviet military leaders found that the Germans had difficulty replacing experienced NCOs (non-commissioned officers) and officers in the field. Taking them out helped to both break the German chain of command and engender a sense of helplessness in the enemy.

Deployed at squad level from Stalingrad onwards, Soviet snipers were estimated to have a 50 per cent probability of hitting a standing, man-sized target at 800m (½ mile), and an 80 per cent probability of hitting a standing, man-sized target at 500m. For distances not exceeding 200m, the probability was estimated to be well above 90 per cent.

The five most famous and successful Soviet snipers were:

Ivan Sidorenko	500 kills
Fyodor Okhlopkov	429 kills
Lyudmila Pavlichenko	309 kills
Nina Lobkovskaya	308 kills
Vasily Zaytsev	225 kills

The hero of Stalingrad, Vasily Zaytsev, chalked up 225 confirmed kills during the battle. The Soviet propaganda machine ensured Zaytsev became a star in the corps of snipers. After Stalingrad, he trained some thirty students in this deadly art; they would go on to kill over 3,000 German soldiers between them.

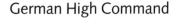

German High Command

 Adolf Hitler (1889–1945) – Chancellor of Germany from 1933 to 1945 and served as head of state as Führer und Reichskanzler. Supreme commander and commander-in-chief of all German armed forces. He committed suicide in April 1945.

 Hermann Goering (1893–1946) – Commander-in-chief of the Luftwaffe and Reichsmarschall of the Wehrmacht. Goering was sentenced to death after the Nuremburg Trials but committed suicide before he could be hanged.

 Joseph Goebbels (1897–1945) – Reich Minister for Propaganda. Goebbels had total control of the German press and radio. He committed suicide in April 1945.

 Heinrich Himmler (1900–45) – Head of the SS, the Waffen SS and Gestapo, and Minister of the Interior. Himmler committed suicide in 1945 after being captured by the Allies.

 Field Marshal Walter von Brauchitsch (1881–1948) – Commander-in-chief of the German army from 1938 until his resignation at the end of 1941. He was arrested and charged with war crimes, but died in Hamburg in 1948 before he could be prosecuted.

 Field Marshal Wilhelm Keitel (1882–1946) – Chief of the high command of the German armed forces (OKW) from 1938 until the end of the war. At the Nuremburg Trials he was found guilty of war crimes and hanged.

 General Alfried Jodl (1890–1946) – Head of the operations section of the OKW. He was found guilty of war crimes at the Nuremburg Trials and hanged.

 Admiral Erich Raeder (1876–1960) – Commander-in-chief of German naval forces until January 1943 when he was replaced by Admiral Doenitz. Raeder was sentenced to ten years' imprisonment for war crimes.

Admiral Karl Doenitz (1891–1980) – Commander of the German navy's U-boats until 1943, then subsequently commander-in-chief of the navy (Oberbefehlshaber der Kriegsmarine) until 1945. Named head of state (Staatsoberhaupt), with the title of President (Reichspräsident), and supreme commander of the armed forces in Hitler's will; he was the last President of the Third Reich. Following the Nuremburg Trials he was sentenced to ten years' imprisonment for war crimes.

Angel in the Centerfold – Ten Soldiers' Pin-Ups

💜 **Andrews Sisters** – The Andrews Sisters were a close-harmony singing group, specialising in swing and boogie-woogie music, which consisting of three real life sisters: LaVerne, Maxene and Patty. During the Second World War they dedicated a huge amount of time to entertaining Allied troops; taking such hits as *Boogie, Woogie Bugle Boy* and *Don't Sit Under the Apple Tree* across America, Africa and Italy, visiting military bases, hospitals, and munitions factories.

💜 **Betty Grable** – Betty Grable's iconic bathing suit photo became the number one pin-up for GIs in the war. It was later included in *Life* magazine's '100 Photos that Changed the World'. She was born Elizabeth Ruth Grable and starred in small parts in over fifty Hollywood movies, before finally hitting the big time in the Cole Porter's *Du Barry Was a Lady* (1939).

💜 **Jane Russell** – More famous with GIs for her magnificent bust than her acting, Jane Russell came to fame in 1943 for her role in the infamous Howard Hughes film *The Outlaw*. The film had actually been released in 1941 but Hughes' exploitation of Russell's less tangible assets had meant that the file was suppressed until 1943 by the censors.

💜 **Rita Heyworth** – Heyworth was a teen nightclub dancer who became a major movie star following a bit part in Howard Hawks' 1939 aviation classic *Only Angels Have Wings*. She was known as the 'Love Goddess', an image which was cemented with Bob Landry's 1941 *Life* magazine photograph of her kneeling on her own bed in a silk and lace nightgown. She became one of the most requested wartime pin-ups.

💜 **Lana Turner** – Turner was a child star who signed to MGM at just 16 and went on to achieve huge fame during the 1940s. She became a popular pin-up girl due to such films such as *Ziegfeld Girl*, *Johnny Eager* and her four films with MGM's 'king of the lot', Clark Gable. Turner even had a B-17 Flying Fortress – the 'Tempest Turner' – named after her.

💜 **Ann Sheridan** – Signed by Paramount Pictures at the age of 19 after winning a beauty contest, Clara Lou Sheridan only achieved stardom after changing her studio (to Warner Bros) and her name (to Ann). The move saw her cast with Jimmy Cagney in *Angels with Dirty Faces*, and from then on she was one of the biggest stars of the '40s. Tagged 'The Oomph Girl', Sheridan was a popular pin-up girl, receiving as many as 250 marriage proposals a week from eager GI fans.

- **Vera Lynn** – Loved more for her voice than her looks, Vera Lynn became 'the Forces' Sweetheart' after the *Daily Express* asked British servicemen to name their favourite musical performers. During the war Lynn had her own radio programme, *Sincerely Yours*, which sent messages to British troops serving abroad. She also toured Egypt, India and Burma, giving outdoor concerts for the troops, for which she later received the Burma Star.

- **Gracie Fields** – Fields was a hugely popular singer and comedienne who signed up for ENSA when war broke out; performing on the backs of open lorries and in war-torn areas as the British Expeditionary Force retreated from the Nazi onslaught. In March 1940 she married Italian-born film director Monty Banks. His Italian citizenship meant the couple were forced to spend the second part of the war in exile in North America or face internment. Nonetheless, Fields continued to spend much of her time entertaining troops outside Britain in Europe and the Pacific.

- **Betty Driver** – Driver was a child star who was singing for the BBC at the age of 10. During the war she joined ENSA and entertained troops throughout Europe with her brand of comedy and big band singing. She also appeared for seven years on the radio show *Henry Hall's Guest Night*. Today, however, she is best known for her role as Betty Turpin on the long-running soap *Coronation Street*.

- **Edith Piaf** – Known as 'The Little Sparrow', this French singer and national icon became globally known during the war for her warbling voice and soulful ballads. Controversially, she performed for both her French audience and the occupying German Forces. While some considered her a traitor, the decision did little to dent her popularity at home or abroad; later she would claim to have been working for the French Resistance.

Animals Go to War

All sides in the war enlisted animals to serve in their armies. The military chose them for their strength and their natural ability to function in hostile terrain. Furthermore, by exploiting these animals' natural instincts, they were even deployed as weapons in themselves. Below is our list of those beasts that served side by side with their human masters in combat:

 Horses

Some 8 million horses were killed in the First World War, but advances in mechanised transport meant they were not such a key element in movement and supply in the Second World War. Nonetheless, most nations still used horse units. The Polish army deployed cavalry to defend against the armies of Nazi Germany during the 1939 invasion. The Soviet Union also maintained cavalry units throughout the war, where the surprise attacks of their Cossack forces were particularly feared on the Eastern Front. British and American forces both used cavalry against the Japanese in the Far East. Indeed, in campaigns in North Africa generals such as George S. Patton lamented the lack of horses, saying: 'Had we possessed an American cavalry division with pack artillery in Tunisia and in Sicily, not a German would have escaped.'

Mules and Donkeys

These sure-footed pack animals were used in countless numbers for their load-bearing abilities in the most difficult terrain, notably on the rocky slopes of Monte Cassino. They also toiled, unflinchingly, in the oppressive heat of Burma, Eritrea and Tunisia to deliver supplies and equipment to front-line forces.

 Dogs

Dogs' intelligence and innate devotion to their masters meant that man's best friend was frequently used to guard vital bases, run messages, lay telegraph wires, detect mines and even to dig out bomb victims. Bizarrely, dogs were also utilised as an anti-tank weapon by Soviet forces, who trained them to carry 256lbs of explosives on their backs and associate the underside of vehicles with food. The Japanese army, meanwhile, were sent some 25,000 dogs from Germany. They attempted to train dogs for demolition using similar Pavlovian techniques as the Soviets. This time, with the hapless hounds pulling carts packed with high-explosive.

 Pigeons

More than 200,000 pigeons were used in the Second World War to carry vital messages; sometimes over long distances when other, more modern methods of communication proved impossible. Flying at the rate of a mile a minute, from behind enemy lines, ships and even aeroplanes, these gallant birds could travel over terrain which prohibited radio waves or human couriers. The Americans even performed experiments to see if pigeons could be used to guide missiles, an eccentric venture known as Project Pigeon.

Other Animals

In the Middle and Far East elephants, camels and oxen were all used for their strength and energy in their native environments. In Europe, amongst the methods of transportation used by the 2nd Polish Corps fighting the Battle of Monte Cassino, was a brown bear called Wojtek, who helped to move boxes of ammunition.

Special Units – The Flying Tigers

- Best known for their infamous shark-faced Curtis P60s, the Flying Tigers was the name given to the 1st American Volunteer Group (AVG) of the Chinese Air Force, who flew between 1941 and 1942.
- Essentially a group of private military contractors, its pilots were recruited under presidential sanction from the United States Army Air Forces (USAAF), Navy (USN) and Marine Corps (USMC), and were commanded by General Claire Lee Chennault.
- The members of the group enjoyed salaries ranging from $250 a month for a mechanic to $750 for a squadron commander; roughly three times what they could have earned in the regular forces. For this reason, the group has sometimes been accused of being little more than mercenaries.

- The Tigers had trained in Burma before the American entry into the Second World War – with the aim of defending China against Japanese forces – and played a significant part in America's propaganda machine.
- They achieved considerable success in the air, with some 300 kills credited to the group; success which was exploited by the US media to boost the nation's confidence in the face of relentless attack by Japanese forces.
- In July 1942, the AVG was replaced by the US Army 23rd Fighter Group, also under General Chennault, which retained the nose art and fighting name of the volunteer unit.

Fleeing the Storm – Air-Raid Shelters

The strategic bombing of UK cities by the Luftwaffe put the British public at grave risk, with falling masonry, flying glass and fire being just as much of a danger to life as the bombs themselves. Despite the fact that an Air-Raid Precautions Committee had been set up in the UK as early as 1924, the country was ill-prepared for the assault to come. In addition to the lack of preparation, relatively few homes in the UK had cellars which might have offered some protection (unlike their European counterparts). As a result, Britain citizens were forced to turn to a series of inventive constructions to shelter from the bombing:

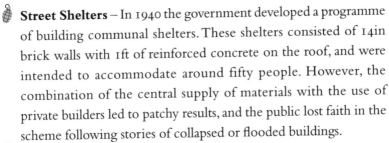

- **Street Shelters** – In 1940 the government developed a programme of building communal shelters. These shelters consisted of 14in brick walls with 1ft of reinforced concrete on the roof, and were intended to accommodate around fifty people. However, the combination of the central supply of materials with the use of private builders led to patchy results, and the public lost faith in the scheme following stories of collapsed or flooded buildings.

- **Anderson Shelters** – The Anderson shelter was designed in 1938 by William Paterson and Oscar Carl (Karl) Kerrison at the request of the Home Office. The shelter was constructed from fourteen curved and straight galvanised corrugated steel panels, and was buried up to 4ft into the ground and covered over with soil. The shelters were 6ft high, 4ft wide and 6ft long, and could hold up to six people. Anderson shelters were issued free to households which earned less than £250 a year, with a nominal charge to higher earners. Some 3.5 million were erected during the war.

- **Morrison Shelters** – The Morrison shelter was designed by John Baker. Unlike the Anderson shelter, the Morrison was to be used indoors and was effectively a table with 8.5in of steel plate on the top and a cage-like construction beneath it – protecting the inhabitants from flying debris. They were approximately 6ft long, 4ft wide and 2ft high. The shelter was provided free to households whose combined income was less than £350 per year. Despite being unable to defend against a direct hit and requiring enough space in the home to erect one, some 600,000 were deployed in the course of the war.

- **Stanton Shelters** – Designed by the Stanton Ironworks in Derbyshire, the Stanton shelter was constructed from several tons of reinforced, interconnected concrete arches bolted in place around a steel frame. Its modular design made large structures relatively cheap and easy to erect for someone with heavy lifting tools, and the shelters were widely used by the Air Ministry.

Underground Stations – Despite their use in the First World War, Whitehall initially tried to discourage people from sheltering in the stations of the London Underground system. However, popular demand soon prevailed and by the autumn of 1940 the tube had become part of the government's 'deep shelter extension policy', with some stations being closed to trains and many being fitted with bunks, canteens, first-aid centres and chemical toilets.

Wartime Lingo – Unusual Nicknames for US Fighting Units

The naming of groups of soldiers in the US army was usually a pretty standard affair, in which the name of the unit indicated its size and purpose and was supported by a number that simply reflected the order in which it had been created. The men who actually fought in these units tended to prefer a nickname that was a little more badass. Below are a few of our favourites:

 The All America – The 82nd US Airborne Division, which saw action in Sicily, Naples, Normandy, the Ardennes, the Rhineland and central Europe.

 First Team – The 1st Cavalry Division – one of the most decorated combat divisions in US army history. They served in the Pacific and occupied Japan for five years at the end of the war.

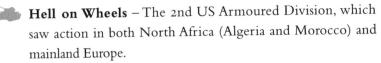

 **Hell on Wheels** – The 2nd US Armoured Division, which saw action in both North Africa (Algeria and Morocco) and mainland Europe.

Spearhead – The 3rd Armoured Division, which was active in Europe during the war. They were also nicknamed the 'Third Herd'.

Screaming Eagles – The US 101st Airborne Division, which was a division of the famous Easy Company that came to fame for its part in the Normandy landings and in the Battle of the Bulge.

Statue of Liberty – The 77th Infantry, which served in the western Pacific, southern Philippines and Ryukyus. They wore a sleeve patch embroidered with the Statue of Liberty.

Iron Horse – The US 4th Infantry Division, which was one of the first divisions to hit the beaches of Normandy on D-Day. They had a second nickname, 'Ivy', a play on words derived from the Roman numerals IV, meaning four.

Pathfinder – The 8th Infantry Division, which saw its first action in July of 1944 during the battle for France, and then across the Rhineland and central Europe.

Texas – The 36th US Infantry Division, which was the first US division to march into mainland Europe, landing at Salerno in Italy.

Thunderbolt – The 83rd Infantry Division, which saw action in Normandy, northern France, the Rhineland, the Ardennes, Alsace and central Europe.

In the Army – Overpaid, Oversexed and Over Here: US Pay

The common soldier has never been that well rewarded for risking his life for his country. A British infantryman in 1940 with no dependants would receive basic pay of around £3 15s per month (approximately £107 in today's money), when he could earn around £6 per month as an unskilled labourer in 'Civvie Street'. While there was a labyrinthine system of special payments for length of service, service classes and skills, as well as supplements for foreign service or service in particular campaigns, the British Tommy was, fundamentally, pretty hard done by.

American soldiers faced a similar disparity between the monies paid to its enlisted men and their earning power out of uniform. To the residents of a near-bankrupt Britain, however, still reeling from the Blitz and the rationing of many day-to-day essentials including food and clothing, the GIs' seemingly limitless cash, along with access to luxuries such as chocolate and nylon stockings, made them look immensely wealthy.

In 1940 the US ranks pulled in the following per month:

$	Master Sergeant and First Sergeant	$138
$	Technical Sergeant	$114
$	Staff Sergeant and Technician Third Grade	$96
$	Sergeant and Technician Fourth Grade	$78
$	Corporal and Technician Fifth Grade	$66
$	Private, First Class	$54
$	Private	$50

In 1940 the dollar exchange rate was pegged by the British government at $4.03 to £1, meaning that the average GI earned four times as much as his British counterpart.

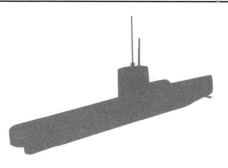

At Sea – Most Successful U-boats

U-boats was the term used for the German submarines (based on U-boot short for *Unterseeboot*, meaning 'undersea boat'), which made up a great deal of Hitler's naval power. There were over 4,000 U-boats commissioned in the war. Despite having a greater range and better firepower than their Allied counterparts, U-boats were primarily either deployed in raiding commercial shipping or hunting in 'wolf packs' to enforce a blockade of the Allied supply lines. These tactics were designed to place Britain in an economic stranglehold. However, as the war went on the U-boats lost their effectiveness and the British navy evolved counter-tactics, taking advantage of a captured Enigma code machine to incept and interpret Nazi communications.

Below are the ten most successful U-boats of the war:

U-48   13 patrols, sunk 51 ships (306,874 tons) and damaged 3 ships (20,480 tons)

U-103   11 patrols, sunk 45 ships (237,596 tons) and damaged 3 ships (28,158 tons)

U-123   12 patrols, sunk 42 ships (219,924 tons) and damaged 6 ships (53,568 tons)

U-124   11 patrols, sunk 46 ships (219,862 tons) and damaged 4 ships (30,067 tons)

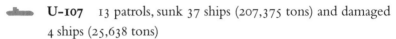

- **U-107** 13 patrols, sunk 37 ships (207,375 tons) and damaged 4 ships (25,638 tons)
- **U-37** 11 patrols, sunk 53 ships (200,124 tons) and damaged 1 ship (9,494 tons)
- **U-66** 9 patrols, sunk 33 ships (200,021 tons) and damaged 4 ships (22,738 tons)
- **U-99** 8 patrols, sunk 35 ships (198,218 tons) and damaged 6 ships (40,101 tons)
- **U-68** 10 patrols, sunk 32 ships (197,453 tons)
- **U-38** 11 patrols, sunk 35 ships (188,967 tons) and damaged 1 ship (3,670 tons)

The Cost of War – 'With Friends Like These, Who Needs Enemies?'

With the forces of so many nations involved in a battles of such huge sizes communication was always a problem and friendly fire could be a real hazard during operations:

- One of the first German servicemen lost in the war was killed by the Japanese, their Axis ally, in China.
- The first American casualty of the war was notched up by the Russians in Finland in 1940.

- The highest-ranking American killed was Lieutenant General Lesley McNair; he fell victim to a USAAF bomb during Operation Cobra as part of the Battle of Normandy.

Probably the most infamous occurrence of friendly fire was the *Cap Arcona* incident. On 3 May 1945 three ships – the *Cap Arcona*, the *Thielbek* and the SS *Deutschland* – were sunk in four synchronised attacks by the Royal Air Force. The action resulted in the death of over 7,000 people. Tragically, their passengers turned out to be Jewish concentration camp survivors travelling with Russian prisoners of war and other survivors of POW camps. The British pilots were unaware that these ships carried POWs, although British documents released in the 1970s stated the Swedish government had informed RAF Fighter Command.

The waters were further muddied by the diverse national make-up of both Allied and Axis forces: citizens of the same country could often find themselves fighting, for pragmatic or political reasons, for either – or even both – sides. Among the first 'German' troops captured by US forces at Normandy were some very confused Koreans who had initially been conscripted into the Japanese army, until they were captured by the Russians and forced to fight for the Red Army. While with the Soviets they were captured by the Germans and, ultimately, forced to fight for them.

Children Go to War – Life in the Hitler Youth

 1926 – It was the Austrian law student Kurt Gruber who brought together disparate right-wing youth movements in Germany to form the Nazi Party's first official youth organisation, the Greater German Youth Movement. Allegedly, it was Rudolf Hess who suggested changing the group's name to Hitlerjugend, Bund deutscher Arbeiterjugend (Hitler Youth, League of German Worker Youth) later in the year.

 1933 – After a series of power struggles the group came under the control of Baldur von Schirach, who became the first Reichsjugendführer (Reich Youth Leader) and went on to enlist over 25,000 boys aged 14 and upwards. Von Schirach made several important changes to the way that the Hitler Youth was organised.

 1936 – Membership of the group was made compulsory for all boys aged 15–18. At the same time, all other youth organisations were banned.

1938 – There were now 8,000 full-time leaders of the Hitler Youth. There were also 720,000 part-time Hitler Youth leaders, often schoolteachers, who had been trained in National Socialist principles. For younger boys aged between 10 and 14 years, von Schirach also set up a new organisation: the Jungvolk.

Apart from providing Adolf Hitler with loyal supporters, the Hitler Youth had a hidden objective: the development of a new Aryan super-race. Favouring those of 'pure Germanic blood', the organisation was essentially a paramilitary one in nature and deeply devoted to Nazi principles. Boys had to take lessons in Nazi dogma as well as more common scouting activities, such as learning semaphore, arms drills and taking part in cross-country hikes. They wore a special uniform and took various tests to rate their skills, before finally being awarded a special dagger marked 'Blood and Honour'.

Girls were also included in the movement but did not receive the same militaristic training. Once girls reached the age of 14 they could join the Bund Deutscher Maedel (German Girls' League) led by Gertrud Scholtz-Klink. They were trained by female guardians in a programme which included a year of farm or domestic service.

The Hitler Youth had it own songs and films, and it published a series of magazines including *Youth and Homeland*, *The Young World*, *The German Girl* and *Girls Your World*. Another magazine, *Will and Power*, was produced for Hitler Youth leaders and female guardians.

During the war the Hitler Youth were often used in air-defence work at home. However, as Germany ran short of soldiers its members were encouraged to join the 12th SS Panzer Division, commanded by Germany's youngest general, Kurt Meyer. As foreign invaders poured into Germany in 1945, members of the Hitler Youth of all ages were armed and told to fight to the death.

In the Army – Types of Weaponry used by Infantry

The Second World War was a uniquely mechanised and technologically sophisticated war. Nonetheless, even with an unprecedented amount of tanks and aircraft in the field, the common foot soldier remained an essential element of all armies. The various classes of weapons carried and used by infantry soldiers are detailed below:

Pistols – Walther P38 (Germany), Luger PO8 (Germany), Nambu pistol (Japan), Beretta model 1934 (Italy), TT30 (Soviet), Webley Revolver (UK), Colt M1911 (US)
Pistols have a short effective range and carry little ammunition, and so were not generally suitable for military combat. They were carried in combat by servicemen who were unlikely to have to use them as their weapon, such as airmen, senior officers and other non-combatant soldiers.

Bolt-Action Rifles – Lee-Enfield SMLE (UK), Mosin-Nagant (Soviet), Arisaka (Japan), M1903 Springfield (US)
When the war began, most soldiers were equipped with bolt-action rifles. These rifles were powerful and accurate weapons, with an effective range of over half a mile. But the slow rate of fire, caused by physically reloading for each shot, meant they were soon outclassed by newer automatic weapons.

Sniper Rifles – SVT-40 (Soviet), Type 97 sniper rifle (Japan)
These were often standard issue bolt-action rifles, which had been produced to higher production standard. Most were specially adapted with magnifying telescopic sights, and in some cases bipods, to maximise the sniper's ability to hit the target at distance.

Semi-Automatic Rifles – AVS-36 (Soviet), M1 Carbine (US)
Semi-automatic rifles were the natural development from the bolt-action rifle. The addition of an automatic reloading mechanism meant these guns provided the soldier with a significantly faster rate of fire, while allowing the shooter keep his aim on the target between shots.

Sub-Machine Guns – Sten Gun (UK), MAS 38 (France), MP40 (Germany), PPSh-41 (Soviet), M3 (US) Thompson M1928A1 (US)

A German invention, evolved from First World War trench warfare, these small, lightweight guns were capable of a rapid rate of automatic fire, and had the advantage of being mechanically simple and very cheap to produce. Their smaller ammunition, similar to that of pistols, meant that a soldier could carry many more bullets than a rifleman, but was hampered by lower range and accuracy. They soon became the weapon of choice for short-range combat and were issued to entire units by the Soviets.

Assault Rifles – M50 Reising (US), FG 42 (Germany), StG 44 (Germany)

These all-purpose guns were developed and used by the German army in the second half of the war. Typically scientific in their approach, the Germans reasoned that, as soldiers almost always fired at enemies when they were closer than half the effective range of a rifle, a compromise between the rifle's range and distance, and the impact of a sub-machine gun, was required. They became the forerunner of modern assault rifles, such as the American M-16 and the Russian AK-47.

Light Machine Guns – M1919 Browning (US), Bren Gun (UK), SG-43 Goryunov (Soviet), Type 97 (Japan), Breda modello 30 (Italy), MG 42 (Germany)

The development of the machine gun had brought mechanised killing to horrifying life in the First World War. With a very rapid rate of fire and a long range, it was an important element in any military unit's firepower. While early versions had essentially been fixed units, the Second World War saw the development of a light machine gun that could be carried by a single soldier, with another soldier carrying additional ammunition, a quick change spare barrel, a tripod and other required parts.

Hand Grenades – M2 (US), No. 36 Mills (UK), F1 grenade (Soviet), Type 97 Hand Grenade (Japan), Model 24 Stielhandgranate (Germany)
Artillery has been an important support weapon since ancient times. The explosive hand grenade was the first weapon that provided foot soldiers with personal and devastating artillery support. Thanks to their simplicity and low production cost, grenades were used widely by all sides in the war. Indeed, during the Battle of Stalingrad some Russian units used only grenades and knives during night-time stealth raids.

Light Mortars – M2 Mortar (US), SBML 2in mortar (UK), Type 89 Grenade Discharger (Japan)
Like machine guns, light mortars are a unit weapon used as self-contained, quick-response artillery able to launch an explosive charge over a maximum range of several hundred meters. Unlike their cousins in heavy artillery support, which was directed by radio instruction, light mortar operators could often see their target, resulting in more precise targeting.

Anti-Tank Weapons – Panzerfaust (Germany), Type 97 (Japan), PTRD-41 (Soviet), PIAT (UK), M1/A1 'Bazooka' (US)
The motorised onslaught of the German blitzkrieg would not have been half so devastating if effective anti-tank weapons had been available in the early stages of the war. Infantry anti-tank weapons began to mature with the development of a hollow

charge warhead, which could impact the target with enough pressure and heat to pierce steel armour. Such warheads could be easily launched by a foot soldier, and were usually fired as a small rocket. Despite their short effective range and low accuracy, they at last gave the infantryman a weapon against tanks.

Flame-Throwers – Flammenwerfer 35 (Germany), Type 100 (Japan), ROKS3 (Soviet), M2 Flamethrower (US)

Yet another German invention from the First World War brought to deadly prominence in the Second Ward War. Flame-throwers became a powerful but very short-ranged weapon (around 30m) for use against a fortified or dug-in enemy. The unit operated by spraying a stream of ignited flammable liquid at the target. However, operating one was in itself dangerous because it immediately revealed the operator's position to counter-fire from enemy forces. This problem was partly solved by the development of flame-thrower tanks, which both protected the operators and carried bigger and more powerful flame-throwers.

Twenty Most Significant Battles of the War

There were many major battles during the war so defining those whose outcome had the most impact is difficult. Some are notable due to heavy losses among the combatants, others for their strategic importance, and others still for their toll on civilian life. Some took weeks to complete, others were over in days or even hours. Below is our selection of the twenty most significant:

- **The Battle of the Atlantic** (September 1939–May 1945) – The Kriegsmarine's (German navy) attempt to destroy the convoys supplying the Allies.
- **The Battle of Britain** (10 July–31 October 1940) – The RAF's victory over the German Luftwaffe.
- **Operation Barbarossa** (22 June–December 1941) – The German invasion of Russia, arguably Hitler's greatest tactical mistake.
- **The Battle of Leningrad** (8 September 1941–27 January 1944) – The siege of the Russian city by German forces was one of the longest and most costly, in civilian lives, of the war.
- **Pearl Harbor** (7 December 1941) – The surprise attack by Japan on American bases in Hawaii that brought the US into the war.
- **The Battle of Midway** (3–6 June 1942) – The Japanese air and sea assault on Midway Atoll, in which Japanese forces were defeated and Pearl Harbor was avenged.
- **The First Battle of El Alamein** (1–27 July 1942) – The attempt by Rommel's Africa Korps to move into Egypt, which, despite victory, failed to achieve dominance in North Africa.
- **The Second Battle of El Alamein** (23 October–4 November 1942) – The Allied counter-attack that ended Nazi ambitions in North Africa.
- **The Battle of Guadalcanal** (7 August 1942–9 February 1943) – The American assault on the Solomon Islands.
- **The Battle of Stalingrad** (21 August 1942–2 February 1943) – The battle for control of the city of Stalingrad that halted the Nazi advance through southern Russia.

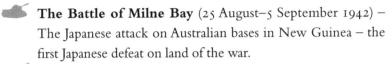

- **The Battle of Milne Bay** (25 August–5 September 1942) – The Japanese attack on Australian bases in New Guinea – the first Japanese defeat on land of the war.
- **Operation Torch** (8–10 November 1942) – The invasion of French North Africa by British and American forces.
- **The Battle of Kursk** (5 July–23 August 1943) – The final German assault on the East which destroyed the core of their Eastern armies.
- **The Battle of Normandy** (6 June–25 August 1944) – The Allied invasion of France – and subsequently Europe – starting with D-Day.
- **The Battle of the Philippine Sea** (19–20 June 1944) – The largest aircraft-carrier battle in history, fought between the Imperial Japanese Navy and the US navy.
- **The Battle of Leyte Gulf** (23–26 October 1944) – The largest naval battle of all time, fought between the Imperial Japanese Navy and the American 3rd and 7th Fleets.
- **The Battle of the Bulge** (16 December 1944–25 January 1945) – The failed German counter-attack against Allied forces in the Ardennes, and their last attempt to turn the tide of the war.
- **The Battle of Berlin** (16 April–2 May 1945) – The Soviet assault on Berlin, which led to the collapse of Germany.
- **The Battle of Iwo Jima** (19 February–16 March 1945) – The American assault on Iwo Jima to disable Japanese air bases and the first attack on Japanese 'home' islands.
- **The Battle of Okinawa** (1 April–21 June 1945) – The largest amphibious assault of the Pacific Theatre, mounted by US Marines against the Ryukyu Islands of Okinawa.

At Sea – Allied Order of Battle at D-Day

D-Day is the name given to the Allied invasion of Normandy on 6 June 1944. A combined airborne and amphibious assault, it remains on the largest amphibious assault ever undertaken in history. British, American, Canadian and Free French forces dropped some 24,000 men into the battlefield by air, while a further 160,000 were landed on French beaches. Below is the order of battle:

 Sword Beach

1st Special Service Brigade comprising No. 3, No. 4, No. 6 and No. 45 (RM) Commandos. No. 4 Commando were augmented by 1 and 8 Troop (both French) of No. 10 (Inter Allied) Commando
I Corps, 3rd Infantry Division and the 27th Armoured Brigade
No. 41 (RM) Commando (part of 4th Special Service Brigade)

 Juno Beach

3rd Canadian Infantry Division, 2nd Canadian Armoured Brigade and No. 48 (RM) Commando
No. 46 (RM) Commando (part of 4th Special Service Brigade)

Gold Beach

XXX Corps, 50th (Northumbrian) Infantry Division and 8th Armoured Brigade

No. 47 (RM) Commando (part of 4th Special Service Brigade)
79th Armoured Division

 Omaha Beach
V Corps, 1st Infantry Division and 29th Infantry Division
2nd and 5th Ranger Battalion

 Utah Beach
VII Corps, 4th Infantry Division and the 359th RCT of the 90th
Infantry Division
101st Airborne Division
82nd Airborne Division

Wartime Heroes – Douglas Bader

Group Captain Sir Douglas Robert Steuart Bader CBE, DSO and
Bar, DFC and Bar, FRAeS, DL (21 February 1910–5 September 1982),
was a Royal Air Force fighter ace who became as well known for
his indomitable attempts at escape as a German POW as his airborne
successes.

 1928 – Bader first joined the RAF in 1928, but he was injured
in an aerobatics crash in 1931 after completing his basic

training. Bader lost both his legs in the crash and, while he attempted to stay in the RAF following his recovery, he was retired for medical reasons in 1933.

1939 – On the outbreak of the Second World War Bader re-enlisted in the RAF. Desperate for experienced pilots, the RAF posted Bader to a fighter squadron where he scored his first kills during the Battle of France, flying Hurricanes. He also enjoyed notable successes during the Battle of Britain where he was a vocal supporter of Trafford Leigh-Mallory's 'Big Wing' experiments, which sought to create leverage in the air by the massed grouping of fighters. He was awarded the Distinguished Flying Cross for his service during the action.

1941 – In March Bader was promoted to wing commander and switched to Spitfires. Now in charge of his own wing Bader proved himself a star pilot, but his leadership proved controversial as he appeared hell-bent on adding to his score of kills and continually badgered his superiors for permission to fly more sorties, even though his men were exhausted.

1941 – In August, disaster struck. Bader was shot down (possibly as a result of friendly fire) and was forced to bail out over German-occupied France. He would spend the rest of the war as a POW. German forces treated Bader with great respect. Having lost one of his prosthetic legs while escaping his aircraft, General Adolf Galland, a former German flying ace, gave the RAF safe passage to drop off a replacement.

1941–45 – While imprisoned, Bader made as much trouble as possible. He immediately attempted to escape from the hospital in which he was recovering. This set the pattern for his time in captivity and his German captors were, ultimately, reduced to confiscating his legs to try to slow him down. He escaped again in August 1942, only to be recaptured and sent to Colditz

Castle. He was eventually liberated by the 1st United States Army in April 1945. He requested a return to action but the request was denied.

1946 – Bader left the RAF permanently in February.

Mid-1950s – His wartime fame resulted in Bader being immortalised in the book and film *Reach for the Sky*.

1976 – Bader was knighted for his services.

In his career, Bader was credited with twenty aerial victories, four shared victories, six probables, one shared probable and eleven damaged. Bader continued to fly and latterly campaigned for the disabled.

Cinema goes to War – Lights, Camera, Action ...

The movie industry began shooting films about the war before it had even ended. Since then there has been a steady stream of celluloid aiming to capture the adventure, tragedy and inspiring heroism of these dark times. It would be simply impossible to make a definitive list of the greatest Second World War movies, not least as they range from Oscar-winning dramas to gritty representations of the horror of war, via 'boys' own adventures' and all-out comedy. Nonetheless, here are a few of our favourites:

Top Ten War Movies Based On Actual Events

The Bridge on the River Kwai (1957, David Lean), starring Alec
Guinness and William Holden

The Longest Day (1962, Ken Annakin), starring John Wayne,
Henry Fonda and Robert Mitchum

Letters From Iwo Jima (2006, Clint Eastwood), starring Ken
Watanabe and Kazunari Ninomiya

A Bridge Too Far (1977, Richard Attenborough), starring Dirk
Bogarde and Michael Caine

Midway (1976, Jack Smight), starring Charlton Heston, Henry
Fonda and Toshiro Mifune

Tora! Tora! Tora! (1970, Richard Fleischer), starring Martin Balsam
and Joseph Cotten

Battle of Britain (1969, Guy Hamilton), starring Michael Caine,
R. Shaw and Laurence Olivier

Battle of the Bulge (1965, Ken Annakin), starring Henry Fonda and
Robert Shaw

Battle of the River Plate (1956, Michael Powell, Emeric
Pressburger), starring John Gregson and Anthony Quayle

Sink the Bismarck (1960, Lewis Gilbert), starring Kenneth More
and Dana Wynter

Top Ten War Biopics

MacArthur (1977, Joseph Sargent), starring Gregory Peck and Ed
Flanders

Patton (1970, Franklin J. Schaffner), starring George C. Scott and
Karl Malden

The Desert Fox (1951, Henry Hathaway), starring James Mason
and Richard Boone

Sergeant York (1941, Howard Hawks), starring Gary Cooper

Schindler's List (1993, Steven Spielberg), starring Liam Neeson
and Ben Kingsley

The King's Speech (2010, Tom Hooper), starring Colin Firth and
Geoffrey Rush

To Hell and Back (1955, Jesse Hibbs), starring Audie Murphy

Downfall (2004, Oliver Hirschbiegel), starring Bruno Ganz and
Alexandra Maria Lara

Enemy at the Gates (2001, Jean-Jacques Annaud), starring Jude
Law and Joseph Fiennes

Reach for the Sky (1956, Lewis Gilbert), starring Kenneth Moore
and Muriel Pavlow

 Top Ten War Action Movies

The Bridge at Remagen (1969, John Guillermin), starring George
Segal and Robert Vaughn

The Dirty Dozen (1967, Robert Aldrich), starring Lee Marvin,
Charles Bronson and Telly Savalas

The Great Escape (1963, John Sturges), starring Steve McQueen
and James Garner

Where Eagles Dare (1969, Brian G. Hutton), starring Richard
Burton and Clint Eastwood

The Guns of Navarone (1961, J. Lee Thompson), starring Gregory
Peck and Anthony Quinn

Von Ryan's Express (1965, Mark Robson), starring Frank Sinatra
and Trevor Howard

Kelly's Heroes (1970, Brian G. Hutton), starring Clint Eastwood
and Donald Sutherland

In Which We Serve (1942, Noel Coward, David Lean), starring
Noel Coward and John Mills

Operation Crossbow (1965, Michael Anderson), starring George
Peppard and Sophia Loren

The Big Red One (1980, Samuel Fuller), starring Lee Marvin,
Mark Hamill and Robert Carradine

 **Top Ten Too Good To Miss**

The Thin Red Line (1998, Terrence Malick), starring Sean Penn and Nick Nolte

Saving Private Ryan (1998, Steven Spielberg), starring Tom Hanks and Edward Burns

Catch-22 (1970, Mike Nichols), starring Alan Arkin and Richard Benjamin

In Which We Serve (1942, Noel Coward, David Lean), starring Noel Coward and John Mills

Das Boot (1981, Wolfgang Petersen), starring Jurgen Procnow

Stalag 17 (1953, Billy Wilder), starring William Holden and Otto Preminger

The Naked and the Dead (1958, Raoul Walsh), starring Aldo Ray and Cliff Robertson

Sink the Bismarck (1960, Lewis Gilbert), starring Kenneth More and Dana Wynter

Flags of Our Fathers (2006, Clint Eastwood), starring Ryan Phillippe and Jesse Bradford

Cross of Iron (1977, Sam Peckinpah), starring James Coburn and James Mason

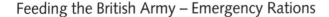

Feeding the British Army – Emergency Rations

The old adage that an army marches on its stomach is certainly true. Any army that is not fed properly is likely to under-perform and, more worryingly, loot the area they're in – which is never popular with the locals in either occupied or liberated territory. When British soldiers couldn't be served by field kitchens they were issued with emergency rations, usually in packs designed to last twenty-four hours. The packs attempted to balance nutrition with compactness, however, the taste of these tinned delights was usually not high on the agenda for those who deigned them.

The ration issued to British troops just before D-Day is listed below. This version contains a tinned pork product much like Spam, but there were seven varieties of the ration featuring other sources of protein, such as chicken and tuna:

- 1 tin of Spam
- 1 pack of biscuits (plain)
- 1 pack of biscuits (sweet)
- 1 pack of instant oatmeal
- 2 packets of meat broth
- 1 block of 'Vitamin Fortified' chocolate
- 1 sachet of boiled sweets
- 2 tea blocks (created from combined tea, milk and sugar)
- 1 pack of matches
- 1 pack of toilet paper
- 2 packs of chewing gum
- 1 pack of sugar tablets
- 1 instruction and menu sheet

If the soldier was lucky these emergency rations might be supported by tinned wet food known as 'Compo'; such rations might include beans, evaporated milk or fruit puddings.

Evacuation!

In 1939 Britain found itself in real and present danger from the encroaching German forces in Europe. Everyone expected cities to be bombed as the Luftwaffe tried to destroy factories and infrastructure, and many feared the gassing of the civilian population. As a result, the Government Evacuation Scheme was implemented in September 1939:

- The scheme had been developed during the summer of 1938 by the Anderson Committee and was implemented by the Ministry of Health. It would see some 3.5 million people evacuated from the cities as part of Operation Pied Piper.
- The plan was put into action with about 800,000 children being moved from their homes in London. Further waves of evacuation occurred from the south and east coasts in June 1940, when a seaborne invasion was expected, and from affected cities after the Blitz expanded in September 1940.
- Child evacuees were despatched to Devon, Cornwall, Wales, East Anglia and Scotland where there was less risk of air raids. Most

went to live with host families where their new homes were called 'billets'. Unless the families had relatives in the area, these placements were usually arranged by 'billeting officers'.

For many children, the evacuation journey began with the same walk to school they took every day. From there buses took them to railway stations and on to their final destination.

Every child was issued with a gas mask, food for the journey (a pack lunch of sandwiches, apples and chocolate) and a small bag for their clothes. Labels recording each child's name, home address, school and where he or she was going were pinned to the children's coats.

While children were the most high-profile of evacuees, the bulk of the programme saw the movement of 524,000 mothers and children under 5, 13,000 pregnant women, 7,000 disabled persons and 103,000 teachers. Civil servants and others vital to the country's infrastructure were also moved.

In addition to the work of the government, many wealthy families chose to evacuate 'privately'; spending the war as residents of hotels in Canada, the US, South Africa, Australia or the Caribbean.

United States High Command

Franklin D. Roosevelt (1882–1945) – President and commander-in-chief of US armed forces. Roosevelt served an unprecedented four terms in office following his election in 1933. He oversaw the rearmament of the US, and introduced the Lend-Lease Act in order to supply Britain and her Allies with weapons and equipment. He died shortly before the end of the war.

Harry S. Truman (1892–1972) – Vice President after replacing Henry Wallace in 1944, he then became President in April 1945 following Roosevelt's death. He took the final decision to use the atomic bomb to the end the war in the East.

Henry L. Stimson (1867–1950) – Secretary of War from July 1940 and a keen international collaborator. Stimson was a supporter of Lend-Lease and the repeal of the Neutrality Act. Stimson also introduced compulsory military service for US nationals. He resigned in September 1945.

Harry Hopkins (1890–1946) – Secretary of Commerce until August 1940 and then the chief diplomatic advisor to Roosevelt. He conferred with Churchill and Stalin on wartime aid requirements and was architect of the Lend-Lease programme.

Cordell Hull (1871–1955) – Secretary of State until November 1944, principally involved with the ill-fated US–Japanese negotiations before Pearl Harbor. He received the Nobel Peace Prize in 1945 for his role in establishing the United Nations.

Edward R. Stettinius Jnr (1900–49) – Succeeded Hull as Secretary of State in November 1944. Stettinius had previously been special advisor to Roosevelt on matters of war production and war economics.

- **Frank Knox** (1874–1944) – Secretary of the navy from 1940. Knox was responsible for the reconstruction and expansion of the US navy following Pearl Harbor. He died in April 1944.
- **Admiral Ernest J. King** (1878–1956) – Chief of Naval Operations (COMINCH-CNO) during the war and member of the Joint Chiefs of Staff. He wrote to Roosevelt in 1944 to say he had reached mandatory retirement age, whereupon he was promoted to the newly created rank of Fleet Admiral.
- **General George C. Marshall** (1880–1959) – Army chief of staff from 1939. Marshall led the expansion of the US armed forces from 130,000 men to a strength of some 8.3 million men, and played a leading role in strategic planning for all theatres of the war. Later, as Secretary of State, he was instrumental in the Marshall Plan – the economic support which rebuilt Europe. He was awarded the Nobel Peace Prize in 1953.
- **Admiral William D. Leahy** (1875–1959) – Chief of Naval Operations from 1937–39, governor of Puerto Rico 1939–40, ambassador to Vichy France 1940–42 and chief of staff to the President from 1942–49.

Actors Who Have Played Adolf Hitler

Adolf Hitler has been justly demonised over the years as a result of the devastation he wreaked on the world. Nonetheless, he was a man of tremendous charisma, an inspiring orator and sometimes a tactical genius. He remains one of the most infamous characters in history and a huge attraction for dramatists. Many actors have played Hitler on large and small screens; either as a demon, a comic figure or in a genuine attempt to capture the man behind the monstrous reputation. Here are just ten of them:

Anthony Hopkins	*The Bunker* (1981)
Bruno Gatz	*Downfall* (2004)
Charlie Chaplin	*The Great Dictator* (1940)
Alec Guinness	*Hitler: The Last Ten Days* (1973)
Stephen Berkoff	*War and Remembrance* (1989)
Liam Neeson	*War Without End* (1996)
Robert Carlyle	*Hitler: The Rise of Evil* (2003)
Alan Cumming	*Jackboots on Whitehall* (2010)
Ian Mckellen	*Countdown to War* (1989)
Derek Jacobi	*Inside the Third Reich* (1982)

Wartime Lingo – Code Names for Successful Military Operations …

In war, knowledge is power. Intelligence on your enemies' movements and numbers could mean the difference between dramatic victory and terrible defeat. As such, both sides feared infiltration by spies and devoted huge resources to gathering intelligence by any means possible. It became standard military practice to ensure the security of your strategic movements by assigning code names to operations. Below are just a few:

- **Operation Cobra** – The American breakout from Normandy, eight weeks after the D-Day landings, as General Omar Bradley took advantage of the German skirmishes with British and Canadian forces around the town of Caen to punch through the German defences.
- **Operation Dragoon** – The successful amphibious invasion of southern France. It paved the way for an Allied force to unite with those who had invaded in the north, and advance towards Germany.
- **Operation Flintlock** – The American invasion of the Marshall Islands in early 1944. It resulted in the Japanese having to withdraw from the Marshall Islands and pushed them back closer to Japan.
- **Operation Lightfoot** – The first British offensive at El Alamein, which was driven back by Erwin Rommel's Africa Korps.
- **Operation Mercury** – The German invasion of Crete. Though successful, this aerial assault was so costly to the Luftwaffe and to German paratroopers who took part that the latter were never employed in an airborne assault again.
- **Operation Overlord** – The Allied invasion of German-occupied Western Europe, also known as the Battle of Normandy. The operation commenced on 6 June 1944 and involved a 12,000-plane airborne assault, preceded by an amphibious assault involving almost 7,000 vessels carrying nearly 160,000 troops.

- **Operation Sturgeon Catch** – The final German offensive on the Balkan city of Sevastopol. The city had held on for several months before a final offensive drove the Russians to surrender.
- **Operation Supercharge** – The heavily reinforced British army's final breakthrough at El Alamein.
- **Operation Torch** – (Initially Operation Athlete.) The Allied invasion of French North Africa in November 1942. The Allies launched amphibious landings in Casablanca, Oran and Algiers before pushing into Tunisia.
- **Operation Uranus** – The Russian offensive to surround the German 6th Army at Stalingrad in November 1942. The Soviets broke through weak Romanian lines to capture some 300,000 Germans and their allies.
- **Operations Yellow and Red** – The pincer movements employed by the German blitzkrieg during the Battle of France in 1940. Yellow saw German armoured units push through the Ardennes, while Red saw German forces outflank the Maginot Line and push deep into France.

… and Code Names for Failed Military Operations

- **Operation Autumn Mist** – The devastating German counter-offensive in the Ardennes Forest in December 1944, also known as the Battle of the Bulge. While a breathtaking success in its first week, the offensive ground to a halt when the Axis armoury ran out of fuel, giving the Allies time to reorganise.
- **Operation Barbarossa** – The German invasion of Russia in 1941. The first year of the invasion saw the German blitzkrieg surge deep into Russian territory, before being halted by the freezing Russian winter.

- **Operation Battleaxe** – A British army offensive against German and Italian forces in eastern Cyrenaica in June 1941. Far from lifting the Siege of Tobruk as generals had hoped, the action saw the British lose over half of their tanks on the first day, before being pushed back by a series of German counter-attacks.

- **Operation Blue** – The German offensive to capture the Russian oil fields in the Caucasus. Despite making early gains, Hitler became sidetracked by the Battle for Stalingrad and the German forces failed to achieve control of an invaluable supply of oil.

- **Operation Citadel** – A German offensive designed to capture the Kursk salient in 1943. The Battle of Kursk remains both the largest armoured clash and the costliest single day of aerial warfare in history. The Germans fought themselves to a standstill across a battlefield the size of Wales. It was the last major offensive mounted by the Germans in the East.

- **Operation Husky** – The Allied invasion of Sicily. While British, Canadian and US airborne forces did achieve their strategic goals, the operation was a disaster for their airborne units, who suffered heavy casualties from friendly fire.

- **Operation Iron Hammer** – A strategic bombing by the Luftwaffe of power generators near Moscow and Gorky. Destroying just two out of three of these turbines could have knocked out 75 per cent of the power used by the Soviet Union. Originally, Germany planned to deploy long-range bombers armed with special floating mines. However, a shortage of bombers and fuel, technical problems with the mines and the rapid Red Army advances meant the plan was postponed and finally dropped.

- **Operation Market Garden** – The Allied offensive to secure a Rhine crossing at Arnhem, Holland in 1944, made famous by the book and film *A Bridge Too Far*.

- **Operation Spring Awakening** – The German offensive against Hungarian oil fields in March 1945. It saw Hitler rashly remove German units from the Ardennes offensive, in an ambitious attempt to capture the last remaining oil fields accessible to German forces. As the Americans rallied against the Germans in the Ardennes, a huge Russian counter-offensive conclusively drove them back in Hungary.

- **Operation U Go** – The Japanese army's attempt to destroy the Allied forces at Imphal and invade India. The offensive culminated in the Battles of Imphal and Kohima, where the Japanese were beaten back by the Allies. Its failure marked the turning point in the Burma Campaign and remains one of the largest Japanese defeats on land of the war.

Wartime Heroes – Recipients of the Victoria Cross

The Victoria Cross (VC) is highest award for valour 'in the face of the enemy' awarded to the British and Commonwealth armed forces. It can be awarded to a person of any rank in any service, and even to civilians under military command. It was named after Queen Victoria who constituted the medal in 1856 as a way to recognise the bravery of those who had served in the Crimean War.

The Victoria Cross was awarded 182 times to 181 people in the war; the anomaly in the numbers being created by New Zealander Charles Upham who received the Victoria Cross and Bar for two separate acts of extraordinary courage. He won his first VC on Crete in 1941 while commanding a platoon in the battle for Maleme Airfield. In the course of a single 3,000yd advance, Upham attacked a German machine-gun nest, killing eight paratroopers, then destroyed another which had been erected in a nearby house. Finally he crawled to within 15yds of a Bofors anti-aircraft gun before destroying it with grenades.

His second VC was earned in 1942, while engaged in the defence of the Ruweisat Ridge in the 1st Battle of El Alamein. Upham charged a position defended by machine-gun fire and hurled grenades into a truck full of German soldiers. Like so many holders of this unique decoration, Upham remained magnanimous about his achievements, saying: 'The military honours bestowed on me are the property of the men of my unit.'

Athur Aaron	No. 218 Squadron RAF	12 August 1943
Michael Allmand	6th Gurkha Rifles	11–23 June 1944
Charles Anderson	2/19th Battalion, AIF	18–22 January 1942
Eric Anderson	East Yorkshire Regiment	6 April 1943
John Anderson	Argyll and Sutherland Highlanders (Princess Louise's)	23 April 1943
Richard Annand	Durham Light Infantry	15 May 1940
Cyril Barton	No. 578 Squadron RAF	30 March 1944
John Baskeyfield	South Staffordshire Regiment	20 September 1944
Sidney Bates	Royal Norfolk Regiment	6 August 1944
Ian Bazalgette	No. 635 Squadron RAF	4 August 1944
Stephen Beattie	HMS *Campbeltown*	27 March 1942

✠ John Beeley	King's Royal Rifle Corps	21 November 1941
✠ Premindra Bhagat	Corps of Indian Engineers	31 January–1 February 1941
✠ Frank Blaker	9th Gurkha Rifles	9 July 1944
✠ John Brunt	Sherwood Foresters (Nottinghamshire and Derbyshire Regiment)	9 December 1944
✠ Richard Burton	Duke of Wellington's (West Riding) Regiment	8 October 1944
✠ Robert Cain	South Staffordshire Regiment	17–25 September 1944
✠ George Cairns	South Staffordshire Regiment	13 March 1944
✠ Donald Cameron	HMS X6	22 September 1943
✠ John Campbell	Royal Horse Artillery	21–23 November 1941
✠ Kenneth Campbell	No. 22 Squadron RAF	6 April 1941
✠ Lorne Campbell	Argyll and Sutherland Highlanders (Princess Louise's)	6 April 1943
✠ Edward Chapman	Monmouthshire Regiment	2 April 1945
✠ Edward Charlton	Irish Guards	21 April 1945
✠ Leonard Cheshire	No. 35 Squadron RAF, No. 76 Squadron RAF, No. 617 Squadron RAF	1940–July 1944
✠ Albert Chowne	2/2nd Battalion, AIF	25 March 1945
✠ Aubrey Cosens	Queen's Own Rifles of Canada	22–23 February 1945
✠ John Cruickshank	No. 210 Squadron RAF	17–18 July 1944
✠ Arthur Cumming	Frontier Force Regiment	3 January 1942
✠ David Currie	South Alberta Regiment	18–20 August 1944

Roden Cutler	Royal Australian Artillery	19 June–6 July 1941
Tom Derrick	2/48th Battalion, AIF	24 November 1943
Fazal Din	10th Baluch Regiment	2 March 1945
Dennis Donnini	Royal Scots Fusiliers	18 January 1945
Thomas Durrant	Corps of Royal Engineers	27 March 1942
George Eardley	King's Shropshire Light Infantry	16 October 1944
John Edmondson	2/17th Battalion, AIF	13–14 April 1941
Hughie Edwards	No. 105 Squadron RAF	4 July 1941
Keith Elliott	22nd Battalion, NZEF	15 July 1942
Harold Ervine-Andrews	East Lancashire Regiment	31 May–1 June 1940
Eugene Esmonde	825 Naval Air Squadron	12 February 1942
Edward Fegen	HMS *Jervis Bay*	5 November 1940
Henry Foote	7th Royal Tank Regiment	27 May–15 June 1942
John Foote	Royal Canadian Army Chaplain Corps	19 August 1942
Ian Fraser	HMS XE3	31 July 1945
John French	2/9th Battalion, AIF	4 September 1942
Christopher Furness	Welsh Guards	17–24 May 1940
Philip Gardner	4th Royal Tank Regiment	23 November 1941
Donald Garland	No. 12 Squadron RAF	12 May 1940
Yeshwant Ghadge	Maratha Light Infantry	10 July 1944
Gaje Ghale	5th Gurkha Rifles	24 May 1943
Guy Gibson	No. 617 Squadron RAF	16 May 1943
James Gordon	2/31st Battalion, AIF	10 July 1941
Thomas Gould	HMS *Thrasher*	16 February 1942
Percival Gratwick	2/48th Battalion, AIF	25–26 October 1942

Robert Gray	HMS *Formidable*	9 August 1945
Thomas Gray	No. 12 Squadron RAF	12 May 1940
John Grayburn	Parachute Regiment	17–20 September 1944
George Gristock	Royal Norfolk Regiment	21 May 1940
George Gunn	3rd Regiment Royal Horse Artillery	21 November 1941
Arthur Gurney	2/48th Battalion, AIF	22 July 1942
Bhanbhagta Gurung	2nd Gurkha Rifles	5 March 1945
Lachhiman Gurung	8th Gurkha Rifles	12–13 May 1945
Thaman Gurung	5th Gurkha Rifles	10 November 1944
Abdul Hafiz	9th Jat Infantry	6 April 1944
Ali Haidar	13th Frontier Force Rifles	9 April 1945
John Hannah	No. 83 Squadron RAF	15 September 1940
Henry Harden	Royal Army Medical Corps	23 January 1945
John Harman	Queen's Own Royal West Kent Regiment	8–9 April 1944
John Harper	York and Lancaster Regiment	29 September 1944
Jack Hinton	2nd Division, NZEF	29 April 1941
Charles Hoey	Lincolnshire Regiment	16 February 1944
Stanley Hollis	Green Howards	6 June 1944
David Hornell	No. 162 Squadron RCAF	24 June 1944
Alec Horwood	Queen's Royal Regiment (West Surrey)	18–20 January 1944
Alfred Hulme	2nd Division, NZEF	20–28 May 1941
Thomas Hunter	43 Commando	2 April 1945
James Jackman	Royal Northumberland Fusiliers	25 November 1941
Norman Jackson	No. 106 Squadron RAF	26 April 1944

Namdeo Jadav	Maratha Light Infantry	9 April 1945
David Jamieson	Royal Norfolk Regiment	7–8 August 1944
Francis Jefferson	Lancashire Fusiliers	16 May 1944
Karamjeet Judge	15th Punjab Regiment	18 March 1945
Richard Kelliher	2/25th Battalion, AIF	13 September 1943
Edward Kenna	2/4th Battalion, AIF	15 May 1945
John Kenneally	Irish Guards	28 April 1943
Geoffrey Keyes	No. 11 (Scottish) Commando	17–18 November 1941
William Kibby	2/48th Battalion, AIF	23–31 October 1942
Bruce Kingsbury	2/14th Battalion, AIF	29 August 1942
George Knowland	No. 1 Commando	31 January 1945
Ganju Lama	7th Gurkha Rifles	12 June 1944
Anders Lassen	Special Air Service	8–9 April 1945
Herbert Le Patourel	Hampshire Regiment	3 December 1942
Nigel Leakey	King's African Rifles	19 May 1941
Roderick Learoyd	No. 49 Squadron RAF	12 August 1940
Ian Liddell	Coldstream Guards	3 April 1945
John Linton	HMS *Turbulent*	September 1939–23 March 1943
David Lord	No. 271 Squadron RAF	19 September 1944
Charles Lyell	Scots Guards	22–27 April 1943
John Mackey	2/3rd Pioneer Battalion, AIF	12 May 1945
James Magennis	HMS XE3	31 July 1945
John Mahony	Westminster Regiment	24 May 1944
Hugh Malcolm	No. 18 Squadron RAF	4 December 1942
Leslie Manser	No. 50 Squadron RAF	30 May 1942
Jack Mantle	HMS *Foylebank*	4 July 1940

✠ Charles Merritt	South Saskatchewan Regiment	19 August 1942
✠ Ron Middleton	No. 149 Squadron RAF	28 November 1942
✠ Anthony Miers	HMS *Torbay*	4–5 March 1942
✠ George Mitchell	Gordon Highlanders	23–24 January 1944
✠ Andrew Mynarski	No. 419 Squadron RCAF	12 June 1944
✠ John Nettleton	No. 44 Squadron RAF	17 April 1942
✠ Augustus Newman	Essex Regiment	28 March 1942
✠ William Newton	No. 22 Squadron RAAF	16–18 March 1943
✠ Moana-Nui-a-Kiwa Ngarimu	28th Māori Battalion, NZEF	26–27 March 1943
✠ Harry Nicholls	Grenadier Guards	21 May 1940
✠ Eric Nicolson	No. 249 Squadron RAF	16 August 1940
✠ Gerard Norton	Kaffrarian Rifles	31 August 1944
✠ John Osborn	Winnipeg Grenadiers	19 December 1941
✠ Robert Palmer	No. 109 Squadron RAF	23 December 1944
✠ Frank Partridge	8th Battalion, AIF	24 July 1945
✠ Frederick Peters	HMS *Walney*	8 November 1942
✠ Basil Place	HMS X7	22 September 1943
✠ Patrick Porteous	Royal Regiment of Artillery	19 August 1942
✠ Tul Pun	6th Gurkha Rifles	23 June 1944
✠ Lionel Queripel	10th Parachute Battalion	19 September 1944
✠ Agansing Rai	5th Gurkha Rifles	26 June 1944
✠ Bhandari Ram	10th Baluch Regiment	22 November 1944
✠ Chhelu Ram	6th Rajputana Rifles	19–20 April 1943
✠ Kamal Ram	8th Punjab Regiment	12 May 1944
✠ Richhpal Ram	6th Rajputana Rifles	7 February 1941
✠ John Randle	Royal Norfolk Regiment	4–6 May 1944
✠ Reginald Rattey	25th Battalion, AIF	22 March 1945
✠ Claud Raymond	Corps of Royal Engineers	21 March 1945

William Reid	No. 61 Squadron RAF	3 November 1943
Peter Roberts	HMS *Thrasher*	16 February 1942
Maurice Rogers	Wiltshire Regiment	3 June 1944
Gerard Roope	HMS *Glowworm*	8 April 1940
Robert Ryder	HMS *Campbeltown*	28 March 1942
Willward Sandys-Clarke	Loyal Regiment (North Lancashire)	23 April 1943
William Savage	HM Motor Gun Boat	28 March 1942
Arthur Scarf	No. 62 Squadron RAF	9 December 1941
Derek Seagrim	Green Howards	20–21 March 1943
Alfred Sephton	HMS *Coventry*	18 May 1941
Sher Shah	16th Punjab Regiment	19–20 January 1945
Robert Sherbrooke	HMS *Onslow*	31 December 1942
William Sidney	Grenadier Guards	8–9 February 1944
Gian Singh	15th Punjab Regiment	2 March 1945
Nand Singh	Sikh Regiment	11–12 March 1944
Parkash Singh	8th Punjab Regiment	6 January 1943
Prakash Singh	13th Frontier Force Rifles	16–17 February 1945
Ram Singh	1st Punjab Regiment	25 October 1944
Umrao Singh	81st West African Division	15–16 December 1944
Ernest Smith	1st Canadian Infantry Division	21–22 October 1944
Quentin Smythe	Royal Natal Carabineers	5 June 1942
Richard Stannard	HMT *Arab*	28 April–2 May 1940
Leslie Starcevich	2/43rd Battalion, AIF	28 June 1945
James Stokes	King's Shropshire Light Infantry	1 March 1945

✠	Sefanaia Sukanaivalu	Fiji Infantry Regiment	23 June 1944
✠	Edwin Swales	No. 582 Squadron RAF	23 February 1945
✠	Lalbahadur Thapa	2nd Gurkha Rifles	5–6 April 1943
✠	Netrabahadur Thapa	5th Gurkha Rifles	25–26 June 1944
✠	Sher Thapa	9th Gurkha Rifles	18–19 September 1944
✠	George Thompson	No. 9 Squadron RAF	1 January 1945
✠	Frederick Tilston	Essex Scottish Regiment	1 March 1945
✠	Frederick Topham	1st Canadian Parachute Battalion	24 March 1945
✠	Leonard Trent	No. 487 Squadron RNZAF	3 May 1943
✠	Lloyd Trigg	No. 200 Squadron RAF	11 August 1943
✠	Paul Triquet	Royal 22e Régiment	14 December 1943
✠	Hanson Turner	West Yorkshire Regiment (The Prince of Wales' Own)	6–7 June 1944
✠	Victor Turner	Rifle Brigade (Prince Consort's Own)	27 October 1942
✠	Charles Upham	2nd Division, NZEF	22–30 May 1941 and 14–15 July 1942
✠	Richard Wakeford	Hampshire Regiment	13 May 1944
✠	Adam Wakenshaw	Durham Light Infantry	27 June 1942
✠	Malcolm Wanklyn	HMS *Upholder*	24 May 1941
✠	Bernard Warburton-Lee	HMS *Hardy*	10 April 1940
✠	James Ward	No. 75 Squadron RAF	7 July 1941
✠	Tasker Watkins	Welch Regiment	16 August 1944
✠	William Weston	Green Howards	3 March 1945
✠	Thomas Wilkinson	HMS *Li Wo*	14 February 1942

| Eric Wilson | East Surrey Regiment | 11–15 August 1940 |
| Peter Wright | Coldstream Guards | 25 September 1943 |

The Cost of War – Cities Under Siege

The concept of laying siege to a city seems almost medieval to the modern mind, but many military fortresses and cities were besieged during the war. In the East:

 Leningrad – Probably the most significant siege of the war, it lasted over twenty-nine months – about half of the length of the war – and saw the death of around 1.5 million combatants.

 Stalingrad – Proved equally deadly.

Sevastopol – This saw the use of the most powerful siege artillery ever used on the battlefield with the German deployment of an 800mm railway gun and a 600mm siege mortar.

In the West:

 Tobruk – Proved remarkably resilient to Axis assaults.

Monte Cassino – Proved remarkably resilient to Allied assaults, indeed the slopes around Monte Cassino became a horrific killing ground.

Malta – This tactically significant island, when besieged by Erwin

Rommel's Africa Korps, proved so courageous under sustained German bombardment that the entire population was awarded the George Cross.

Arguably, mechanisation and the importance of movement in modern warfare have meant that the practise of siege is on the decline. During the blitzkrieg the awesome French Maginot Line was simply bypassed by German forces, and battles that would have taken place around cities were replaced with bombing campaigns or air assaults by paratroops. However, air power was also proven to be invaluable to those under siege: such as new air-bridge methods, which were developed and used extensively in the Burma Campaign for supplying the Chindits under siege in Imphal, German forces in the Demyansk Pocket, and, less successfully, at Stalingrad.

Top Operations – Fortitude: Hiding the Goodies

In 1943, Operation Roundup saw the Allies transfer a large part of the Anglo-American military forces to England in preparation for a full-scale invasion of mainland Europe. Allied high command knew that troop movements on such a scale would not go unnoticed by the occupying Axis forces in Europe, so the Allies came up Operation Fortitude – one of the largest counter-intelligence bluffs ever mounted.

The plan was simple: to convince the Germans that the invasion would not occur in Normandy, and hence avoid them filling the area with reinforcements. The operation was divided into Fortitude North – designed to fool the Germans into believing the plan was to invade Norway – and Fortitude South – designed to have them believe that the main invasion of France would occur in the Pas-de-Calais.

The overall strategy for the deception was directed by the London Controlling Section and involved six key tactics:

- **Inflatable Tanks and Boats** – The Allies built inflatable lures which, when seen from reconnaissance aircraft, were believed to be real units. The south-east of England was dotted with thousands of fake tanks, transport vehicles and artillery, painted with the marks of the 3rd Army. While in the harbour at Dover, wooden or rubber warships were docked.
- **Staged Aerial Reconnaissance** – The Royal Air Force was ordered to allow German reconnaissance aircraft to fly freely over key areas of southern England. They did, however, continue to shoot down enemy bombers.
- **Distraction Air Raids** – Air-raid activity was intensified in the north of France. For example, on the night of 5/6 June 1944, several thousand tons of bombs were dropped in the Pas-de-Calais region.
- **False Signals and Messages** – A flotilla of small boats was sent into the English Channel to emit false radio signatures.
- **Controlled Intelligence** – The Allies released allegedly secret information through a network of German and Italian double-agents.
- **Appearances by Key Staff** – Key military personal, notably General George W. Patton, commander of the 3rd Army, made public appearances to support the ruse.

Twenty Most Deadly Battles of the War

The loss of any human life is always a tragedy. So in a conflict that saw the deaths of 60 million servicemen and women, and some of the largest battles the world had ever known on land, in the air and at sea, it seems a little churlish to try to quantify the greatest losses of the conflict. Nonetheless, the battles below are ranked for their deadly nature based on the losses of the forces committed to the field:

 The Battle of Kursk (July–August 1943) – The largest tank battle ever fought. It occurred when German forces aimed to capture sixty-six Soviet divisions, whose combination of skill and fortification turned an onslaught into a battle of attrition. The battle ended in stalemate as Germany lost 100,000 killed/wounded/captured and the Soviet Union lost 250,000 killed and 600,000 wounded.

The East Prussian Offensive (January–August 1944) – The Soviet Union launched this massive offensive to destroy 100 German divisions guarding Prussia and Poland. Hitler, as always, refused his troops permission to withdraw and the German Army Centre was totally destroyed. Germany lost 800,000 killed/wounded/captured and the Soviet Union lost 1.3 million killed/wounded.

The Battle of Stalingrad (August 1942–February 1943) – Probably the greatest and most brutal urban battle ever fought; the unstoppable force of the German blitzkrieg met the immovable object of Soviet resolve. Germany lost 300,000 killed/wounded/captured and the Soviet Union lost 1.2 million killed.

The Battle of Berlin (January–April 1945) – The Soviet drive towards Berlin saw them battle the remains of the Wehrmacht and Waffen-SS, as well as many Volkssturm and Hitler Youth, as the German nation made its last stand. Germany lost 200,000 soldiers and as many civilians killed, and the Soviet Union lost 600,000 killed/wounded.

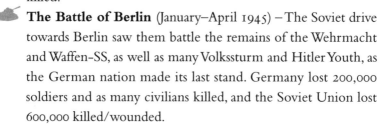 **The Battle of Normandy** (June–September 1944) – This battle saw the amphibious invasion of France and the fierce fighting that followed as the British, American and Canadian troops broke out of Normandy and the Allies drove the Germans back village by village. Germany lost 216,000 killed/wounded/captured and the Allies lost 209,000 killed/wounded/captured.

The Battle of Moscow (October 1941–January 1942) – The German drive towards the Russian capital was slowed by skilful Soviet counter-attack, before the under-supplied invaders ground to a halt as the severe winter storms closed in. Germany lost 200,000 killed/wounded/captured, and the Soviet Union lost 700,000 killed/wounded/captured.

The Battle of the Bulge (December 1944–January 1945) – The supremely daring last-ditch German counter-attack that caught the Allies unaware and only faltered as German supplies ran low. Germany lost 100,000 killed, and the US and UK lost 82,400 killed/wounded/captured.

The Battle of the Atlantic (September 1939–May 1945) – A five-year-long battle as German submarines attempted to disrupt supply ships going to England and the Soviet Union. Germany lost 50,000 naval officers killed and the Allies lost 50,000 merchants and sailors killed.

The Battle of Britain (July 1940 to October 1940) – The Luftwaffe's attempt to destroy the RAF before an invasion of England was thwarted by superior use of tactics and RADAR by the British. Germany lost 3,000 pilots killed and England lost 1,800 pilots killed.

The Battle of France (May–June 1940) – The German blitzkrieg assault of France through Belgium and Holland neatly sidestepped the French army and sent the ill-prepared British and Belgium armies towards a disastrous evacuation from Dunkirk. France lost 350,000 killed/wounded, England lost 100,000 killed/wounded with 40,000 captured, and Germany lost 100,000 killed/wounded.

The Battle of Midway (June 1942) – The Japanese attempt to overrun US bases on the island of Midway, resulting in the greatest aircraft-carrier battle of the war. A total disaster for Japan; they lost four aircraft carriers and 3,500 sailors killed, and the US lost one and 500 sailors killed.

The Battle of Leyte Gulf (25 October 1944) – Arguably the largest naval battle of all time. Japan's attempt to destroy US transport ships carrying troops and supplies to the Philippines ended in near total annihilation of the Imperial Navy. Japan lost over 10,000 sailors killed and the US just 2,000 sailors killed.

The Battle of Imphal (March–June 1944) – Japan's attempt to invade India was repelled by British and Indian troops fighting around the city of Imphal. Around 30,000 British and Indian soldiers were killed/wounded, while 80,000 Japanese troops died before the remainder were driven back into Burma.

The Battle of Okinawa (April–June 1945) – The US attempt to invade the island of Okinawa as a steppingstone to an assault on Japan. This resulted in such brutal fighting the US chose to deploy an atomic bomb against Japan, rather than risk repeating a similar battle. Japan lost 120,000 soldiers killed defending the island, and the US had 58,000 casualties.

The Battle of West Hunan (April–June 1945) – The battle between the Japanese and Chinese to control the Chinese supply lines and airfields in Hunan province. China lost over 300,000 soldiers killed and Japan lost 60,000 soldiers killed. Despite these heavy losses, China continued to drive the over-extended Japanese into retreat.

The Battle of Poland (1 September–6 October 1939) – The battle that began the war saw the ill-equipped Polish army pitch cavalry against tanks. The invading German and Russian forces then portioned the country between them. Germany lost 3,000 killed and Poland lost 100,000 soldiers killed/wounded.

The Battle of Burma (19 March–1 May 1945) – The Japanese defeat at the Battle of Burma ended the Japanese threat to India, and paved the way for the Allies to supply China through Burma. This was the last battle that the British army was involved in during the Second World War. Japan lost 40,000 soldiers killed and Allied forces lost 6,000 killed.

The Battle of the Philippines (20 October 1944–3 March 1945) – The battle ended after the fall of Manila in very heavy street fighting. Japan lost nearly 150,000 soldiers killed and 200,000 Filipino civilians killed – 100,000 in Manila alone – the US had 30,000 casualties.

The Battle of Guadalcanal (7 August 1942–6 March 1943) – One of the largest naval, marine and army engagements in the Pacific Theatre. The Japanese defeat at Guadalcanal ended their dominance in the South Pacific. Japan lost 70,000 killed/wounded/captured, and the Americans suffered 30,000 casualties and 10,000 killed.

The Battle of Anzio (23 January–25 May 1944) – The Allied attempt to the end stalemate in Italy failed in the Battle of Anzio. The American forces were trapped for four months in this pocket until troops broke through the German defences in Italy and linked up with Anzio. Anzio was perhaps the biggest Allied blunder in the Second World War. Germany lost 100,000 killed/wounded/captured and the Allies lost 135,000 killed/wounded/captured.

The Battle of El Alamein (23 October–3 November 1942) – The defeat of the German army in Egypt signalled the end of the Axis empire in North Africa. Germany and Italy lost 60,000 troops killed, with 30,000 being taken prisoner. The British lost 25,000 men killed/wounded.

The Battle of Tunisia (14 February–12 May 1943) – The cornered German and Italian forces in Tunisia launched a final attack against the Americans at Kasserine Pass, which defeated the US forces. The Allies soon recovered and forced a gradual retreat of German forces back to the sea. The Allies sustained 45,000 casualties in their conquest of Tunisia, with 10,000 killed. Germany and Italy lost 300,000 troops: 275,000 taken prisoner and 25,000 killed/injured.

The Battle of Seelow Heights (10–15 April 1945) – The last German defence before Berlin. Germany lost 80,000 killed/wounded/captured and the Soviet Union lost 200,000 killed/wounded.

The Battle of Iwo Jima (19 February–25 March 1945) – The most intense, bloody and compact battle in the Pacific Theatre. With over 100,000 US soldiers fighting 25,000 Japanese on a

small island. In the end, the US had 30,000 casualties and Japan had 20,000.

 The Battle of Manchuria (8–16 August 1945) – The Soviet Union, after defeating Germany, declared war on Japan and launched a massive attack on Japanese troops in the Chinese province of Manchuria. The Russians suffered 5,000 casualties and 80,000 Japanese soldiers were killed or injured.

In the Army – Equivalent Ranks in the German and British Forces

German	British
Gemeiner, Landser	Private
Grenadier	Lance Corporal
Obergrenadier	–
Gefreiter	Corporal
Obergefreiter	–
Stabsgefreiter	–
Unteroffizier	Sergeant
Unterfeldwebel	Colour Sergeant
Feldwebel	–
Oberfeldwebel	Sergeant Major

Stabsfeldwebel	–
–	Warrant Officer
Leutnant	Second Lieutenant
Oberleutnant	First Lieutenant
Hauptmann	Captain
Major	Major
Oberstleutnant	Lieutenant Colonel
Oberst	Colonel
–	Brigadier
Generalmajor	Major General
Generalleutnant	Lieutenant General
General	General
Generaloberst	–
Generalfeldmarschall	Field Marshal

Special Units – Desert Rats

- Identified by the distinctive Desert Rat divisional flash they wore, the men of the Western Desert Force were legendary for their tenacity and toughness against overwhelming odds.
- The Desert Rats were a British mobile armoured force formed from the Cairo Cavalry Brigade (three armoured regiments: the

7th, 8th and 11th Hussars) and the 1st Royal Tank Regiment (RTR), supported by 3rd Regiment Royal Horse Artillery (RHA) and a company of Royal Army Service Corps (RASC).

- At the time of the Italian declaration of war in 1940, many of these troops had been serving in the area for two years without leave. Even worse, the unit was meant to be equipped with 220 tanks when they actually had just sixty-five, many of them the near obsolete Vickers Medium Mark II. The Rats found themselves alone, under-armed and massively outnumbered. Despite the odds, the Italians proved to be no match for the British and they captured some 250,000 Italians.

- Rommel's Afrika Korps would prove to be a different proposition however and, despite well-deserved reinforcements, the Rats found themselves embroiled in back-and-forth fighting for the possession of Tobruk in the brutal heat of the desert for the next year.

- While Rommel's superior tactics would ultimately hold the Rats at bay, the Western Desert Force would go on to become a vital component of Montgomery's Eighth Army. As part of this larger force, the Rats took part in most of the major battles of the North African Campaign – including both Battles of El Alamein – and made an historic contribution to the allied victory in North Africa.

Japanese High Command

 **General Hideki Tojo** (1884–1948) – Thought to be largely responsible for the attack on Pearl Harbor, Tojo was a general in the Imperial Japanese Army (IJA) who became the 40th Prime Minister of Japan in 1941. A near dictator, he held many concurrent positions in the Japanese government including Army Minister and Home Minster. As the tide of the war changed against the Japanese, Tojo fell from grace and eventually resigned in 1944. After his resignation he attempted to commit suicide but survived, only to be tried for war crimes by the Allies and hanged in 1948.

 **Lieutenant General Kuniaki Koiso** (1880–1950) – A career soldier who was appointed Prime Minister after the fall of Tojo in 1944, Koiso was a token prime minister as he was not allowed to interfere in military decisions and, ultimately, resigned in April 1945. He was tried for war crimes by the Allies and spent the rest of his life in prison.

 **Baron Kantaro Suzuki** (1867–1948) – An admiral in the Imperial Japanese Navy, Suzuki became Prime Minister in April 1945 after the collapse of Koiso's leadership. It was he who finally persuaded Emperor Hirohito to surrender to the Allies. Suzuki resigned after the surrender was announced.

 **General Yoshijiro Umezu** (1880–1949) – Commander-in-chief of the Kwangtung Army from 1939–44. He was promoted to Chief of the Imperial Japanese Army General Staff in 1944 and signed the Japanese surrender aboard the USS *Missouri* in 1945. He was tried as a war criminal and sentenced to life imprisonment in 1948.

 **Admiral Isoroku Yamamoto** (1884–1943) – Japanese Naval Marshal General and commander-in-chief of the Combined

Fleet. Yamamoto was the architect of the Japanese carrier forces but was killed when his aircraft was ambushed by the Americans in April 1943.

Women Go to War

The Second World War continued the precedent set by the First World War, in which women were employed to take over vital roles in military administration, agriculture, the civil service and industry vacated by male soldiers at the front. Despite the circumstances, many women found their wartime roles intensely liberating, as between the wars women had been restricted to working in domestic service or junior positions in education, medical or secretarial roles – jobs which they usually retired from when they married.

By the end of the war there were some 460,000 serving women in the military and over 6.5 million women in civilian war work. It was a marked difference in Nazi Germany, where Hitler had forbidden women from working in weapons factories as he felt that a woman's place was at home. Here are just some of the ways in which the 'fairer sex' contributed:

The Women's Land Army (WLA)

As in the First World War, women were called on to help on the land and the Women's Land Army (WLA) was reformed in July 1939. By August 1940 only 7,000 women had joined, but the threat to the country's supply lines posed by Hitler's U-boat blockade instigated a huge drive to increase domestic food production. Government propaganda used to recruit women to the WLA tried to make the work look glamorous. In fact, the work was hard and often saw young women posted in isolated communities and billeted in farm workers' cottages without running water, electricity or gas.

Factory Work

Some women chose to replace their husbands, fathers and sons working in local factories, while other female volunteers were forced to relocate to be closer to their designated workplace. Women worked in all manner of production and often made ammunition, weapons and uniforms used at the front. As with their WLA counterparts, the hours worked in factories were long, a situation that was exacerbated by the fact that they were often paid less than their male counterparts.

The Women's Voluntary Service (WVS)

During the Blitz women in voluntary organisations played their own unique role supporting those on the home front. The WVS had 1 million members by 1943, many of whom were elderly. The WVS provided tea and refreshments for those who sheltered in the Underground during the Blitz, and for the fire-fighters who worked to clear up the wreckage left by the Luftwaffe assault on the surface. The WVS also knitted socks, scarves and balaclavas for servicemen.

Military Service

In 1943, the shortage of men in factories led to the government stopping women joining the armed forces and giving them only the choice of either working on the land or in the factories. However in the first half of the war, all three services were open for women to join:

 Auxiliary Territorial Service (ATS) – In the army, women joined the Auxiliary Territorial Service. Like soldiers they wore a khaki uniform, but unlike soldiers, were seldom issued with a weapon. They generally served as drivers, worked in mess halls and acted as cleaners. Some manned and maintained anti-aircraft guns, but an order f rom Winston Churchill himself forbade any woman from actually firing an anti-aircraft gun; he felt women would not be able to cope with the knowledge that they might have killed someone.

 The Women's Auxiliary Air Force (WAAF) – In the Royal Air Force (RAF), women joined the Women's Auxiliary Air Force. Like their army colleagues they did the same cooking, clerical and cleaning work. Many also operated the new RADAR stations, tracking incoming enemy aircraft – a dangerous role in itself as the stations were key targets for air attack. Some women also trained as pilots – though their duties usually only extended to flying new planes from the factory to the squadron base.

 The Women's Royal Naval Service (WRNS) – In the Royal Navy (RN), women joined the Women's Royal Naval Service. The WRNS had initially been formed in 1917. They generally served as cooks, clerks and secretaries, though others did work as telegraph operators, electricians

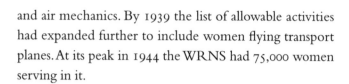

and air mechanics. By 1939 the list of allowable activities had expanded further to include women flying transport planes. At its peak in 1944 the WRNS had 75,000 women serving in it.

Evacuation and Entertainment

Women also played their part in less quantifiable roles. Millions of children were evacuated from cities considered to be in danger of Luftwaffe attack. Mothers with young children were evacuated together but many older children went with their teacher, usually a woman. Women also served as air-raid wardens. Importantly, the morale of the country also depended heavily on women. The two most famous female entertainers of the war were Vera Lynn and Gracie Fields. Known as the 'Forces Sweetheart', Vera Lynn's songs, such as *There'll be Blue Birds Over the White Cliffs of Dover* and *We'll Meet Again*, brought great hope to the beleaguered people of Britain.

Wartime Lingo – Quotations from Generals

When great bodies of men and women are locked in conflict, it often takes the words of great leaders to inspire action and explain the higher purpose of the unimaginable horrors that must be endured. For members of the public this role largely fell to politicians, but soldiers on the front line always looked to their generals for inspiration:

- **Fleet Admiral Chester W. Nimitz** – 'Among the men who fought on Iwo Jima, uncommon valour was a common virtue.'
- **Admiral Halsey** – 'Before we're through with them, the Japanese language will be spoken only in hell!'
- **General Dwight D. Eisenhower** – 'I hate war as only a soldier who has lived it can, only as one who has seen its brutality, its futility, its stupidity.'
- **Arthur 'Bomber' Harris** – 'They have sown the wind … now they shall reap the whirlwind.'
- **Admiral Yamomoto** – 'I fear all we have done is awakened a sleeping giant and filled him with a terrible resolve.'
- **Gen. MacArthur** – 'We are not retreating – we are advancing in another direction.'
- **Field Marshal Bernard Montgomery** – 'Discipline strengthens the mind so that it becomes impervious to the corroding influence of fear.'

Feeding the German Army – Emergency Iron Rations

While on campaign, German soldiers were served hot meals once a day from their company or battalion field kitchen. Normally, soldiers would be issued with a bread ration every day – typically *Kriegsbrot*, a dark, multi-grain bread. In addition they would receive cheese, preserves and sausage in the morning. A hot stew was prepared at lunch while supper was again based around the bread ration, with the addition of instant soup.

When out of range of a field kitchen, German troops were issued with a pre-packaged emergency ration called the Iron Ration. The full Wehrmacht Iron Ration consisted of:

- 300g of hard crackers (*Zwieback*, *Hartkeks* or *Knäckebrot*)
- 200g of preserved meat (*fleischkonserve*)
- 150g of preserved or dehydrated vegetables (*gemüse*), or pea sausage (*erbsenwurst*)
- 25g of artificial substitute coffee (*Kaffe-Ersatz*)
- 25g of salt (*salz*)

While the full Iron Ration was stored in a field kitchen wagon, there was also the half-Iron Ration (*halb-eisernes*) which was carried by each soldier and consisted of tinned meat and crackers only. To supplement the *halb-eiserne* portion, there might also be soup (*Wehrmachts-Suppe*) and coffee.

Unlike their Allied counterparts, German soldiers could not even depend on the Iron Ration. As the war progressed, German forces had their supply lines so severely disrupted that soldiers at the front were often left to forage for their own dinner.

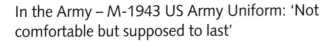

In the Army – M-1943 US Army Uniform: 'Not comfortable but supposed to last'

Far from the stylish martial designs enjoyed by Allied colleagues and Axis enemies, American combat uniforms tended to be pragmatic and minimalist. They were created from a combination of wools and herringbone-twilled cotton, and were relatively free of regimental insignia. They often did not even display rank markings – a situation which was necessitated by the GIs' need to pick up replacement clothing in the field.

In 1942, in an attempt to standardise a variety of specialist uniforms and unsuitable garments worn by its enlisted men, the US army began the development of the M-1943 uniform. The results where far from perfect, however. Designed to be worn in layers, the uniforms were hot when they needed to be cool and cold when they needed to be warm, and the lightweight materials did not provide adequate water protection. Workmanship was also an issue, as the wool and khaki used did not have satisfactory locking stitches – trousers were prone to split, while the overalls issued to paratroopers tended to tear at the knees and elbows.

Ongoing problems with issued clothing meant that GIs were inclined to wear a variety of non-regulation items that did perform. Particularly prized were the winter 'tanker' jackets issued to armoured troops and the high-lace Corcoran jump-boots worn by paratroops. In their favour, the uniforms were designed with a lot of pockets which, given the battle-hardened GIs' penchant for discarding non-essential equipment in favour of additional ammo, was seen as an asset.

A new GI was issued with the following:

- M-1943 field jacket and hood
- Pile field jacket

- Field trousers
- Field trouser liner (dropped)
- Field cap
- Pile cap
- High-neck sweater
- M-1943 combat service boots
- M-1943 goggles
- Field pack (a redesigned 'Jungle Pack')
- M-1943 entrenching tool and carrier
- Pocket, cartridge, Cal .30, M1, carbine or rifle
- Rain poncho
- Wool sleeping bag and case
- M3 gas mask (along with its M6 carrier)

One of the most valued items of equipment issued to the American GI was the 1lb steel helmet. This was used for a variety of purposes in the field, including as a washbasin, cooking cauldron, digging tool and even as a weapon in hand-to-hand combat.

Soviet High Command (*Stavka*)

 Joseph Stalin (1879–1953) – The first general secretary of the Communist Party of the Soviet Union's Central Committee from 1922 until his death in 1953. Though nominally elected by the time of the war, Stalin was essentially a dictator who pursued a ruthless policy of deploying his own men as cannon fodder in the face of the German assault on Russia.

Viacheslav Molotov (1890–1986) – A former Bolshevik who served as Minister for Foreign Affairs from 1939 to 1949. Instrumental in the signing of non-aggression pacts with both Germany and Japan, he was equally influential in negotiation with the Allies.

Marshal Alexander Vasilevsky (1895–1977) – After serving as a captain in the First World War, Vasilevsky went on to become Chief of General Staff of the Soviet armed forces and Deputy Minister of Defence during the Second World War. He drove back the Germans in the West and accepted the surrender of the Japanese in the East.

Marshal Georgy Zhukov (1896–1974) – Deputy commander-in-chief of the Red Army. Zhukov directed the defence of Moscow against the German army in 1941 and was instrumental in organising the successful Soviet counter-offensive which destroyed the invading Nazi forces.

Lavrenty Beria (1899–1954) – Head of Soviet intelligence organisation the NKVD. Beria was responsible for propaganda, while simultaneously administrating sections of the Soviet state and acting as de facto Marshal of the Soviet Union, in command of the NKVD field units deployed against partisans and Soviet citizens alike.

Marshal Boris Shaposhnikov (1882–1945) – One of the few Red Army commanders with formal military training, he briefly served as Chief of General Staff before retiring due to ill health in 1941.

Georgy Malenkov (1902–88) – A trained engineer who was promoted to the State Defence Committee (GKO) in 1941

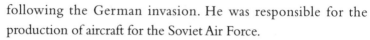

following the German invasion. He was responsible for the production of aircraft for the Soviet Air Force.

Admiral Nikolai Kuznetsov (1902–74) – An Admiral of the Fleet and hero of the Soviet Union; he saved the Soviet navy by predicating Operation Barbarossa and spent much of the war defending the Black Sea from the German navy.

Colonel General Aleksandr Novikov (1900–76) – Commander of the Red Army air force (VVS) throughout the war, Novikov was also author of many innovative aviation and combat techniques. Despite his massive contribution to the Soviet victory, he was accused of treachery by Beria at the end of the war and imprisoned until Stalin's death in 1955.

Marshal Semyon Timoshenko (1895–1970) – Created People's Commissar for Defence and a marshal of the Soviet Union in May 1940. Timoshenko was demoted after the failure of early Soviet counter-attacks, but later redeemed himself in the eyes of Stalin by his dogged defence of Stalingrad.

Big, Bigger, Biggest

- **Biggest Tank** – The heaviest tank ever built was the German Maus II (Panzerkampfwagen VIII). The super-heavy tank was completed in late 1944 and weighed in at 200 metric tons. It was

10.2m (33ft 6in) long, 3.71m (12ft 2in) wide, 3.63m (11.9ft) tall and armed with a 128mm KwK 44 gun. However, by the end of the war it had never reached an operational state.

- **Biggest Guns** – Schwerer Gustav and Dora were the names of two massive German 80cm K (E) railway guns. Developed in the late 1930s by Krupp for destroying heavy fortifications, they weighed nearly 1,350 tons and could fire shells weighing 7 tons to a range of 37km (23 miles). Both Gustav and Dora were deployed in the Soviet Union, notably at the siege of Sevastopol.

- **Biggest Bombs** – The two nuclear weapons used by the United States near the end of war remain the single most destructive device deployed. On 6 August 1945, a uranium-type device codenamed 'Little Boy' was detonated over the Japanese city of Hiroshima. Three days later, on 9 August, a plutonium implosion-type device codenamed 'Fat Man' was exploded over Nagasaki, Japan. These two bombings resulted in the deaths of approximately 200,000 Japanese people – mostly civilians – from injuries sustained from the explosions.

- **Biggest Battle** – The Battle of Kursk represents both the largest tank battle and the single costliest day of aerial combat ever fought. In a battlefield spread over an area the size of Wales, Germany had grouped some 900,000 soldiers, 10,000 artillery guns, 2,700 tanks and 2,000 aircraft. The Soviet forces numbered around 3 million soldiers, 20,000 artillery pieces, 3,600 tanks and 2,400 planes. Fought in two stages between the 4 July and 23 August 1943, nearly 1 million men were killed, wounded or captured.

- **Biggest Ship** – The Japanese battleship INS *Yamato* was the largest battleship of the war. Measuring 263m in length, the ship's displacement was 65.027 tons (including 21 tons of armour). It was propelled by twelve Kanpon boilers driving four turbines:

creating 153.553hp and giving a top speed of 27 knots. Manned by a crew of 2,700 officers and men, the INS *Yamato* boasted nine 18in main guns, 6in secondary guns, twenty-four anti-aircraft guns and seven planes. Despite her huge firepower the ship saw virtually no combat, and was sunk in 1945 by American carrier-based bombers and torpedo bombers.

Firestorm – Ten Devastating Bombing Raids

- **The Second Great Fire of London** (29–30 December 1940) – A devastating night of heavy bombing raids during the Blitz, in which a firestorm raged through the City and other parts of London.
- **The Bombing of Stalingrad** (23–26 August 1942) – The aerial assault of Stalingrad by the Luftwaffe ahead of their ground assault. The bombing killed 955, wounded 1,181 and reduced the city to rubble.
- **The Bombing of Hamburg** (27 July 1943) – The Allied strategic bombing of shipyards, factories and U-boat pens in the German port left 42,600 dead and 37,000 wounded.
- **The Bombing of Kassel** (23 October 1943) – The Allied strategic bombing of armament and aircraft factories created a fire that burned for seven days and killed 10,000.
- **The Bombing of Darmstadt** (11 September 1944) – An attack by the RAF on the mostly wooden medieval town of Darmstadt.

It saw bombers fan out across the city to spread the payload, and resulted in the destruction of the centre of the town and 12,300 dead.

- **The Bombing of Dresden** (13 February 1945) – The Allied bombing of armament factories in Dresden saw 3,600 planes drop as many as 650,000 incendiaries on the city, creating a firestorm that killed as many as 45,000 people.
- **The Firebombing of Tokyo** (9 March 1945) – Known for being one of the most destructive single bombing raids in history the USAAF's firebombing. The Japanese capital, largely built from wood, saw massive destruction and the deaths of 120,000.
- **The Firebombing of Kobe** (17 March 1945) – The American B-29 bomber attack on the centre of Japan's aviation industry destroyed 3 square miles of the city and killed 8,841.
- **The Atomic Bombing of Hiroshima** (6 August 1945) – The USAAF dropped the nuclear device 'Little Boy' on the city, killing 90,000 – many of those as a result of radiation attendant to the nuclear explosion.
- **The Atomic Bombing of Nagasaki** (9 August 1945) – The USAAF dropped a second nuclear device, 'Fat Man', on Nagasaki, killing 60,000 and essentially ending the war.

Five New Tactical Advances – Pushing the Boundaries

The Airlift

The capability to quickly move a large volume of supplies, equipment and personnel to a particular position was used in the war to support advances, or supply troops trapped being enemy lines. The USAAF successfully completed the largest airlift of the war in May 1942, when it moved more than 500,000 tons of cargo from India to China over the Himalayas. In contrast, the airlift technique notably failed when the Luftwaffe attempted to supply the besieged 6th Army in Stalingrad. Goering promised Hitler he could deliver 500 tons of supplies a day. However, the Russian winter meant that no more than 100 tons were ever delivered and beleaguered soldiers soon ran out of food and ammunition.

Strategic Bombing

Between 1939 and 1945 the Allies dropped 3.4 million tons of bombs. The intensive bombing of civilian areas was one of the most controversial aspects of the war, with some still arguing that incidents such as the terrifying firestorms created in Dresden and Darmstadt constitute a war crime. Even though the lines between tactical bombing, to destroy infrastructure and industry, were often blurred with the less justified 'punishment' or 'terror' bombing of civilians, to destroy morale on the ground, all sides took part in strategic bombing at some point during the war. Spurred on by their air supremacy and a reluctance to sustain military casualties on the ground, Allied air forces in both Europe and the Pacific took part in larger and more brazen attack on cities in Germany and Japan, culminating in the dropping of nuclear bombs on Nagasaki and Hiroshima.

Aeronautical Warfare at Sea

Actions such as the attack on Pearl Harbor made it clear that the tactics of maritime warfare were changing. At the start of the war, many had expected the balance of power at sea to lie with mighty battleships and dreadnoughts of old, however, it soon became clear that the carrier would established itself as the dominant capital ship in a fleet. Attacks using fighters, bombers and torpedo bombers launched from aircraft carriers vastly increased the range of attack for maritime vessels. Indeed, the Battle for the Coral Sea was the first naval battle in history in which neither side's ships sighted or fired directly upon the other. In addition to this, many mighty battleships found themselves dangerously vulnerable to attack from the air, with Goliaths such as the INS *Yamato*, HMS *Prince of Wales* and the SMS *Tirpitz* all taken down by air attack.

 ## Use of Tanks

The concept of 'total war' – the synchronised deployment of air power, troops and armoured support – came to devastating fruition with the German blitzkrieg. Whereas the First War World had seen static, trench-based combat, these new tactics relied on increased mobility and combined arms. In this era, the tank moved from being an instrument of infantry support to a primary weapon. Throughout the war tanks grew bigger, faster and more deadly, and the technology used to destroy them therefore became key. By the end of the war, both the American and Soviet forces boasted huge mechanised divisions which would play a key part in the balance of power in Europe during the Cold War.

 ## Use of Paratroops

The use of paratroops allowed attacking forces to seize a tactical advantage, by inserting troops behind enemy lines or to avoid direct assaults on fortifications. German Fallschirmjäger units made the first airborne attack when invading Denmark, on 9 April 1940, as part of Operation Weserübung. British and American forces also made extensive use of parachute drops during the Normandy Landings and later advances into the Rhine Valley. Though they were usually elite units, paratroops did have their disadvantages and were prone to finding themselves under-supplied and dangerously isolated behind enemy lines. As a result, assaults could be as disastrous as they could be decisive: their use by the Germans in the Battle of Crete resulted in large casualties, as did Operation Market Garden, in which British paratroopers attempted an over-ambitious attack the bridge at Arnhem.

At Sea – In which we Serve: Battleships Sunk

⬤ **Sunk in Ship-to-Ship Combat**
HNoMSA *Eidsvold* – Sunk by German destroyers in Narvik Harbour, 9 April 1940
HNoMSA *Norge* – Sunk by German destroyers in Narvik Harbour, 9 April 1940
French Battleship *Bretagne* – Sunk by Royal Navy (RN) warships at Mers-el-Kebir, 3 July 1940
HMS *Hood* – Sunk by the SMS *Bismarck* in the Battle of the Denmark Straight, 24 May 1941
INS *Kirishima* – Sunk by USS *Washington* off Guadalcanal, 15 November 1942
SMS *Scharnhorst* – Sunk by HMS *Duke of York* and cruisers HMS *Belfast*, HMS *Jamaica* and HMS *Norfolk* off Norway,

26 December 1943

INS *Fuso* – Sunk by USS *Melvin* in the Battle of Leyte Gulf,
25 October 1944

INS *Yamashiro* – Sunk by six US battleships in the Battle of
Leyte Gulf, 25 October 1944

Sunk by Combined Ship-to-Ship and Air Attack

SMS *Bismarck* – Sunk by a combination of RN torpedo
bombers, battleships and destroyers, 27 May 1941

SMS *Tirpitz* – Sunk by RN mini-subs, RN aircraft and RAF
bombers in Tromso Harbour, 12 November 1944

Sunk by Submarine

HMS *Royal Oak* (Japan) – Sunk by U-47 in Scapa Flow Naval
Base, 14 October 1939

HMS *Barham* (Japan) – Sunk by U-331 off Sollum,
25 November 1941

INS *Kongo* (Japan) – Sunk by USS *Sealion* off Formosa,
21 November 1944

Sunk by Air Attack in Open Waters

Greek Battleship *Kilkis* – Sunk by German Ju-87 bombers in
the Salamis Channel, 23 April 1941

Greek Battleship *Limnos* – Sunk by German Ju-87 bombers in
the Salamis Channel, 23 April 1941

HMS *Repulse* – Sunk by Japanese aircraft off Malaya,
10 December 1941

HMS *Prince of Wales* – Sunk by Japanese aircraft off Malaya,
10 December 1941

HNLMS *De Zeven Provincien* – Sunk by Japanese bombers off
Surabaya, 18 February 1942

INS *Hiei* – Sunk by US navy and USAF aircraft off Guadalcanal, 13 November 1942

Italian Battleship *Roma* – Sunk by Luftwaffe glider bombs, 9 September 1943

INS *Musashi* – Sunk by US navy aircraft during the Battle of Leyte Gulf, 24 October 1944

INS *Yamato* – Sunk by US air attacks off Okinawa, 7 April 1945

Sunk by Air Attack while at Anchor

Italian Battleship *Conte di Cavour* – Sunk by RN aircraft in Taranto, 11 November 1940

Russian Battleship *Murat* – Sunk by the German bombers in Kronstadt Harbour, 22 September 1941

USS *Oklahoma* – Sunk by Japanese aircraft in Pearl Harbor, 7 December 1941

USS *Arizona* – Sunk by Japanese aircraft in Pearl Harbor, 7 December 1941

USS *California* – Sunk by Japanese aircraft in Pearl Harbor, 7 December 1941

USS *West Virginia* – Sunk by Japanese aircraft in Pearl Harbor, 7 December 1941

SMS *Schleswig-Holstein* – Sunk by RAF bombers in Gotenhaven Harbour, 19 December 1944

Pocket Battleship *Lutzow* – Sunk by Tallboy bombs in Swinemunde, April 1945

Pocket Battleship *Admiral Hipper* – Sunk by RAF bombers in Kiel, 9 April 1945

Danish Battleship *Niels Juel* – Sunk in Eckenforde by allied bombing, 3 May 1945

INS *Haruna* – Sunk by USAF bombers in Kure, 28 July 1945

INS *Ise* – Sunk by USAF bombers in Kure, 28 July 1945

Sunk by Other Means

HMS *Queen Elizabeth* – Sunk by Italian frogmen in Alexandria Harbour, 18 December 1941

HMS *Valiant* – Sunk by Italian frogmen in Alexandria Harbour, 18 December 1941

SMS *Schlesien* – Sunk by mine and Soviet bomber attack; scuttled near Swinemunde, 5 May 1945

INS *Mutsu* – Mysteriously exploded in Oshima Bay, 8 June 1943

Finnish Battleship *Ilmarinen* – Sunk by minefield after shelling Estonian coastal islands, 13 September 1941

The Application of Science – Code Machines

For all sides in the war, the ability to transfer sensitive military data around the world was paramount. Whether this was details of troop movements, the strength of forces, potential targets or the location of key personnel, breaches in security could mean the deaths of thousands. As a result, a covert war was waged between the makers of encryption technology and the code-breakers who tried to decode the algorithms, known as ciphers, which they used to conceal messages. Here is our list of the most important:

Enigma

The first Enigma machine was invented by a German engineer, Arthur Scherbius, at the end of the First World War. This revolutionary device went on to become, probably, the most famous covert device of the war. An Enigma machine is the generic name given to any member of a family of electro-mechanical rotor machines used for the encryption and decryption of secret messages. The machine was available with various modifications; the German armed and intelligence forces adopting their own design – the Enigma G – as early as 1928. British mathematicians, working at Bletchley Park as part of Project Ultra, would partially decode the Enigma cipher with the aid of Polish intelligence. However, their breakthrough only became complete in May 1941, when the Britain captured the German submarine U-110 with its encryption equipment intact.

M-209

Designed by Boris Hagelin, the M-209 was another mechanical rotor-based cipher machine used by the US army. The M-209 was simple, and hence cheap, and was designed to be rugged enough to be used in battlefield conditions. By the end of the war over 140,000 had been made, with the US navy using their own version, the CSP-1500. Its cipher was eventually broken by the Germans in 1943, by which time the US forces – aware of this possibility – had already restricted its use to solely tactical messages.

The Purple Machine

The Japanese *97-shiki O-bun In-ji-ki* ('Alphabetical Typewriter 97') was also based on the same rotor technology as the Enigma machine. To distinguish it from other ciphers used by the

Japanese, it was known to the Allies as the 'purple' machine, after the colour of the folders that the Allied code-breakers used to store their decryptions in. Despite the Japanese refusal to believe it was possible, the cipher was broken by a team from the US Army Signals Intelligence Service, directed by William Friedman, in 1940.

Interestingly, the most secure cipher of the war was amazingly low-tech: the language of the Navajo Indians. It simply involved Navajo servicemen, who were attached to US forces, broadcasting messages in their own tongue. The speed and security of this simple 'cipher' was unmatched by the technological innovations from any country. The Navajos played a major role in every major battle of the Pacific from mid-1942 to the end of the war.

Kamikaze!

Towards the end of war, the tide had turned against Japanese forces in the Pacific. A series of military and naval defeats had driven the Japanese back, a situation compounded by their loss of aerial supremacy due to outdated aircraft and a lack of experienced pilots. With an assault on Japan becoming ever more likely, the Japanese began a series of suicide attacks against Allied shipping in October 1944. These kamikaze (meaning 'divine wind') pilots would attempt to crash planes loaded with explosives into enemy ships, particularly aircraft carriers. Though desperate and obviously costly in men and machines, this last-ditch attempt to cripple the advancing Allied navy was considered important enough to warrant the sacrifice. For nearly a year, the Imperial Japanese Navy (IJN) and Air Force (IJAAF) bombarded Allied forces with kamikaze attacks. In the end, the IJN had sacrificed 2,525 pilots and the IJAAF 1,387. Below is a list of Allied warships sunk by kamikaze attack:

	USS *St. Lo* (CVE-63)	25 October 1944
	USS *Abner Read* (DD-526)	1 November 1944
	USS *Mahan* (DD-364)	7 December 1944
	USS *Ward* (DD-139)	7 December 1944
	USS *Reid* (DD-369)	11 December 1944
	USS *Ommaney Bay* (CVE-79)	4 January 1945
	USS *Long* (DD-209)	6 January 1945
	USS *Bismarck Sea* (CVE-95)	21 February 1945
	USS *Dickerson* (DD-157)	2 April 1945
	USS *Bush* (DD-529)	6 April 1945
	USS *Colhoun* (DD-801)	6 April 1945
	USS *Emmons* (DD-457)	6 April 1945
	USS *Mannert L. Abele* (DD-733)	12 April 1945
	USS *Pringle* (DD-477)	16 April 1945
	USS *Swallow* (AM-65)	22 April 1945
	USS *Little* (DD-803)	3 May 1945
	USS *Luce* (DD-522)	4 May 1945
	USS *Morrison* (DD-560)	4 May 1945
	USS LSM(R)-190	4 May 1945
	USS LSM(R)-194	4 May 1945
	USS *Bates* (DE-68)	25 May 1945
	USS *Drexler* (DD-741)	25 May 1945

	USS *William D. Porter* (DD-579)	10 June 1945
	USS *Twiggs* (DD-591)	16 June 1945
	USS *Barry* (DD-248)	21 June 1945
	USS LSM-59	21 June 1945
	HMS *Vestal* (J215)	26 July 1945
	USS *Callaghan* (DD-792)	29 July 1945

Royalty Goes to War

King George VI was three years into his reign when war broke out in 1939. At this time, English kings had not led their troops into battle since George II at the Battle of Dettingen in 1743, and George VI was no exception. However, he courageously did his part as an inspiring and unflinching figurehead:

- He remained in Buckingham Palace throughout the Blitz even after the building sustained nine direct hits.
- He and his wife, Queen Elizabeth, would tour many of the areas that had suffered from heavy bombing to further express their solidarity with their embattled subjects.
- He founded the George Medal and the George Cross to honour the 'many acts of heroism performed both by male and female persons especially during the present war'. One of the nation's highest awards for extreme bravery (the Victoria Cross being the

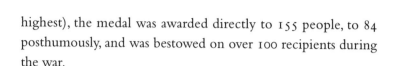

highest), the medal was awarded directly to 155 people, to 84 posthumously, and was bestowed on over 100 recipients during the war.

Other members of the Royal family were more directly engaged in the war effort:

- **Princess Elizabeth** – When evacuated to Windsor Castle she enrolled as a driver in the Auxiliary Territorial Service (ATS). Though the future queen did not see action on the front, she did her part maintaining jeeps.
- **Lord Louis Mountbatten** – More active command was given to Mountbatten, who commanded a flotilla of destroyers and saw considerable action in the Mediterranean. In May 1941, his flagship HMS *Kelly* was sunk by German dive bombers off the coast of Crete with the loss of more than half the crew. Mountbatten ended the war as the Supreme Allied Commander of the South-East Asia Command, working with General William Slim. He also represented Great Britain in receiving the Japanese surrender of Singapore in 1945.

Wartime Lingo – On the QT: A List of Wartime Abbreviations

In times of war, the state plays a huge part in the running of the country. With the government dealing with wartime production, conscription, rationing and the aftermath of air attacks, a range of new national departments and local positions of responsibility were required to keep the country running, fed and safe. Not unsurprisingly, this new infrastructure brought with it a host of new definitions, many of which needed to be issued with an appropriate abbreviation to allow their employees to communicate quickly and clearly. Here is a list of the most common:

A.A.	Anti-Aircraft
A.B.	Assistance Board
A.B.H.	Advanced Base Hospital
A.C.E.	Assistant Chief Engineer
Admty	Admiralty
A.M.	Air Ministry
A.M.W.R.	Air Ministry War Room
A.P.	Armour Piercing (or Anti-Personnel)
A.R.C.C.	Assistant Railway Control Officer
A.R.P.Control	Air Raid Precautions Control or Controller
A.R.P.O. Sub-control	Air Raid Precautions Officer
A.R.P.	Air Raid Precautions Sub-Control or Controller
A.10	Class I Road, No. 10
B. of E.	Board of Education
B.50	Class II Road, No. 50
B. of T.	Board of Trade
Cas.	Casualty, or casualties when word is used alone
C.Clk.	County Clerk
C.C.	County Council
C.Control	Country Control or Controller

C.C.Stn.	Casualty Clearing Station
C.D.	Civil Defence
C.E.	Chief Engineer
Ch.Const.	Chief Constable
C.M.O.	Chief Medical Officer
C.R.F.O	Chief Regional Fire Officer
C.R.H.	Casualty Receiving Hospital
C.R.O.	Chief Regional Officer
C.W.R.	Cabinet War Room
D.A.B.	Delayed Action Bomb
D.A.S.	Department of Agriculture for Scotland
D.B.D.	Director of Bomb Disposal
D.C.	District Commissioner
D.C.E.	Deputy Chief Engineer
D.C.O.	Divisional Coal Officer
D.F.O.	Divisional Food Office or Officer
D.H.S.	Department of Health for Scotland
D.O.O.	Duty Operations Officer
D.R.E.	Divisional Road Engineer
D.T.M.	Director of Torpedoes and Mines
D.T.O.	District Transport Officer
E.C.	Electricity Commission
E.Cttee.	Emergency Committee
E.H.S.	Emergency Hospital Scheme
E.I.O.	Emergency Information Officer
E.R.Cttee	Emergency Repairs Committee
F.	Fragmentation
F.C.R.	Fire Control Room
F.F.	Fire Force
F.F.C.	Fire Force Commander
F.O.I.C.	Flag Officer in Charge

⬤	Gaselec.	Gas and Electricity Deptment
⬤	G.H.Q.	General Headquarters
⬤	G.I.O.	Gas Identification Officer
⬤	G.P.	General Purposes
⬤	G.P.O.	General Post Office
⬤	G.V.	Goods Vehicle
⬤	H.D.E.	Home Defence Executive
⬤	H.E.	High Explosive
⬤	H.G.V.	Heavy Goods Vehicle
⬤	H.O.	Home Office
⬤	HOFOR.	Home Forces
⬤	H.S.W.R.	Home Security War Room
⬤	H.Q.	Headquarters
⬤	I.B.	Incendiary Bomb
⬤	I.G.	Inspector General
⬤	K.P.C.R.	Key Points Control Room
⬤	K.P.I.B.	Key Points Intelligence Branch
⬤	K.P.I.O.	Key Points Intelligence Officer
⬤	L.A.	Local Authority
⬤	L.I.S.	Land Incident Section
⬤	L.O.	Liaison Officer
⬤	M. of A. & F.	Ministry of Agriculture and Fisheries
⬤	M.A.P.	Ministry of Aircraft Production
⬤	M. of F.	Ministry of Food
⬤	M.G.	Machine Gun
⬤	M. of H.	Ministry of Health
⬤	M.H.S.	Ministry of Home Security
⬤	M.L.O.	Military Liaison Officer
⬤	M. of L.	Ministry of Labour
⬤	M.O.	Medical Officer
⬤	M.O.H.	Medical Officer of Health

M. of I.	Ministry of Information
Mines.	Mines Department
M. of P.	Ministry of Pensions
M. of Supply.	Ministry of Supply
M.T.C.	Mechanised Transport Corps
M. of W.T. (I.T.)	Ministry of War Transport (Inland Transport)
M. of W.T. (Sh)	Ministry of War Transport (Shipping)
N.D.	No Damage
N.F.S.	National Fire Service
O.B.	Oil Bomb
O.O.W.	Operations Officer of the Watch
P.D.R.	Police Duty Room
Pet.	Petroleum Department
P.L.O.	Pension Liaison Officer
P.M.	Parachute Mine
P.O.	Principal Officer
P.O.L.O.	Post Office Liaison Officer
R.A.F.L.O.	Royal Air Force Liaison Office
R.C.	Regional Commissioner
R.C.A.	Regional Communications Adviser
R. & E.	Research and Experiments Department
R.D.	Rural District
R.F.S.O.	Regional Fire Staff Officer
R.I.O.	Regional Information Officer
R.L.O.	Railway Liaison Officer
R.M.O.	Resident Medical Officer
R.O.	Regional Officer
R.P.S.O.	Regional Police Staff Officer
R.S.L.O.	Regional Security Liaison Officer
R.T.A.	Regional Technical Adviser
R.T.C.	Regional Technical Commissioner

R.T.I.O.	Regional Technical Intelligence Officer
R.T.O.	Railway Transport Officer
R.W.A.	Regional Works Adviser
R.X.	Red Cross
S.A.P.	Semi-Armour piercing
Scot.Office.	Scottish Office
S.E.D.	Scottish Education Department
S.G.A.	Senior Gas Adviser
S.H.D.	Scottish Home Development
S.N.O.	Senior Naval Officer
S.R.O.	Senior Regional Officer
S. of S.	Secretary of State
S.S.O.	Senior Staff Officer
S.U.X.A.P.B.	Small Unexploded Anti-Personnel Bomb
S.Y.U.X.B.	Small Yellow Unexploded Bomb
T.Clk.	Town Clerk
T.C.	Town Council
T.E.	Telephone Exchange
U.X.A.A. shell	Unexploded Anti-Aircraft Shell
U.X.B.	Unexploded High Explosive Bomb
U.X.G.B.	Unexploded Gas Bomb
U.X.I.B.	Unignited Incendiary Bomb
U.X.P.M.	Unexploded Parachute Mine
U.X.T.M.G.	Unexploded Type G. Mine
W.A.E.C.	War Agricultural Executive Committee
W.O.	War Office
W.V.S.	Women's Voluntary Service

Fleeing the Storm – Forced Migrations and Evacuations

Conflict on the scale of the Second World War saw the mass movement of people right across the globe. Such movements were usually the result of a tactical retreat by overwhelmed troops, or attempts by civilians to flee the conflict. However, the war also saw the recruitment of forced labour, political persecution on a huge scale and the strategic defence of resources. Below is a list of the most significant:

Evacuations of Military Forces
Operation Dynamo saw the evacuation of the British Expeditionary Force from Dunkirk, France in 1940.
Operation Alphabet saw the evacuation of Allied (British, French and Polish) troops from Norway in 1940.
Evacuation of Soviet troops occurred during the Siege of Odessa by German and Romanian troops in 1941.
Operation Hannibal saw German troops evacuated from East Prussia in 1945.

Emergency Evacuations of Civilians
Key personnel, women and children were evacuated from British cities during the Blitz in 1940.
The population in the western Soviet Union was evacuated after Operation Barbarossa, as the Soviets followed a 'scorched earth' policy by destroying everything behind them.
Finnish children were evacuated to Sweden and Denmark ahead of the Russian invasion in 1941.
Evacuation of Soviet citizens occurred during the Siege of Leningrad by German troops in 1941.
Civilians were evacuated from major cities in Japan during American bombing in 1945.

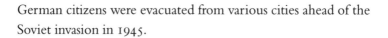

German citizens were evacuated from various cities ahead of the Soviet invasion in 1945.

Forced Migration, Persecution and Internment

Ukrainians, Belarusians and Russians were deported to Germany for use as forced labour between 1941 and 1943.

Jews, prisoners of war and political prisoners were deported to Nazi concentration camps in Germany and German-occupied Poland from 1933 to the end of the war.

Japanese Americans were interned by the US government.

Evacuations of Industry and Infrastructure

The Soviet Union moved most of its industries from the western Soviet Union to the remote areas of the Urals, central Asia, Kazakhstan and the Caucasus to avoid the capture of vital resources by advancing German troops.

The Cost of War – Nations that Sustained the Most Casualties

The Second World War dwarfed all the conflicts before it in its size and scale, but also in the sheer number of military and civilian lives lost. Indeed, to this day no one really knows the actual numbers of those killed. While countries in all parts of the world sustained losses, below is the tragic list of those that suffered most:

✟ **The Soviet Union** – The Soviet Union began the war in a non-aggression pact with Germany. Following Germany's invasion of Russia they joined the Allied effort to crush Nazism.

Soldiers (Allied)	13,300,000 killed
Soldiers (Axis)	408,000 killed
Civilians	6,500,000 killed

✟ **Germany** – Germany was part of the Axis throughout the war.

Soldiers (Axis)	3,350,000 killed
Civilians	3,043,000 killed

✟ **China** – From 1939 to 1941 China was solely at war with Japan. Thereafter it was an Allied partner.

Soldiers (Nationalist)	1,500,000 killed
Soldiers (Communist)	500,000 killed
Civilians	11,500,000 killed

✟ **Japan** – Japan was neutral until its attacks on Pearl Harbor in 1941. Thereafter it aligned itself with the Axis.

Soldiers (Axis)	1,926,500 killed
Civilians	393,000 killed

✟ **Poland** – Between 1939 and 1945 the country was first an Allied partner, then under German occupation and, finally, fought again as an Allied partner.

Soldiers (Allied)	320,000 killed
Soldiers (Axis)	35,000 killed
Partisans	97,000 killed
Civilians	2,900,000 killed

Five Legendary Fighters of the USAF

P-40 Tomahawk – Made famous by the Flying Tiger volunteers fighting in China, the Curtis P-40 was commonly used by the USAF in the early years of the war. Designed to engage enemy planes in air-to-air combat, the P-40 carried heavy machine guns but had little to back them up in terms of speed and manoeuvrability. As a result, it found itself largely outclassed by the infamously nimble Japanese Zero.

P-38 Lightning – Named the 'fork-tailed devil' by the Luftwaffe, the Lightning was a unique twin-engine fighter with an unmistakeable twin-boom design. It was used for ground attack and low-level bombing, and was also fast enough to engage enemy fighters on its own terms. Indeed, top US air ace Richard Bong used this aircraft to shoot down a staggering forty Japanese planes.

P-51 Mustang – Arguably the best propeller-driven fighter of the Second World War, the Mustang was a living example of the Anglo-American alliance: it boasted a British Rolls-Royce Merlin engine fitted into an American-designed airframe. The subsequent output from the propeller was reputedly so powerful that pilots could risk flipping the aircraft upside-down on the runway during take-off. Mustangs could outrun, outshoot and outmanoeuvre almost anything they ran into, and, with the addition of external fuel tanks, could escort allied bombers deep into enemy territory.

F6F Hellcat – Designed as a replacement for the F4F Wildcat, the first Hellcats saw action in 1943 and immediately showed themselves to wildly outclass the Japanese Zeros. In addition to the superior firepower and armour of the Wildcat, the Hellcat had a speed and dexterity that was very close to that of the Zero. The Hellcat proved to be the most successful aircraft in naval history, destroying 5,271 aircraft.

F4U Corsair – Designed as a carrier-based plane, the need to be able to stow its wings resulted in its unique 'gull-wing' design. Though initially sceptical, marine and naval pilots came to love this big, well-armoured aircraft which was almost as manoeuvrable as the Zero and considerably faster. Another candidate for the best fighter of the war, it remained in service into the Korean War.

Feeding the US Army – Emergency Rations

The K-ration was the daily food ration given to soldiers serving in the United States army. Like the British 'compo' ration, it was a highly calorific, balanced meal intended to supplement fare from field kitchens. It was designed for mobile forces such as paratroops, tank crews and couriers, but, in actuality, pretty much all infantry had recourse to K-rations at one time or another.

- **The Breakfast Unit** – This contained a canned entrée of ham and eggs or veal loaf, a cereal bar or dried fruit, instant coffee, biscuits and sugar cubes, as well as Halazone water purification tablets, four cigarettes and chewing gum.
- **The Dinner Unit** – This contained a canned entrée of processed cheese, ham, or ham and cheese; biscuits; fifteen malted milk tablets or five caramel candies; a powdered juice drink which could have been lemon, orange or grape flavour; sugar cubes; a packet of salt; four cigarettes; a box of matches and chewing gum.
- **The Supper Unit** – This contained a tinned main meat course of pork luncheon meat with carrot and apple, chicken paté, beef and pork loaf or sausages; biscuits; a bouillon soup cube or powder packet; a chocolate bar; four cigarettes; chewing gum and a packet of toilet paper tissues.

The most valued part of the ration was the 2oz of chocolate – known as a D-ration. The bar was produced by the Hershey Company who also produced, for those serving in the jungle and desert, the Tropical Bar, which was less likely to melt in the heat. To GIs in the field, chocolate was a welcome luxury and could even be traded for other goods.

Wartime Heroes – British Campaign Medals

Campaign medals were issued to soldiers, sailors, airman and civilians who had served for a specific period under hostile fire in a theatre of war. Unlike the gallantry medals, such as the George Cross or Victoria Cross, where the recipient was nominated for a specific act of bravery, campaign medals were awarded to anyone who qualified. If more than one bar had been awarded, usually the first gained prevailed. Where that service had been cut short by death or a disability, the medals were usually awarded automatically.

No one person was allowed to receive more than two medals, however, in a war as long as the Second World War many service personnel saw action in multiple campaigns. In these cases, bars and clasps were issued to further indicate the individual's service or contribution to notable battles within a campaign.

The King's Medal

The King's Medal was issued in two versions: the King's Medal for Courage in the Cause of Freedom, and the King's Medal for Service in the Cause of Freedom:

The King's Medal for Courage in the Cause of Freedom was introduced on 23 August 1945, to mark the acts of courage by foreign civilians who served the British cause. It was primarily intended to reward foreign civilians who had assisted British escapees in enemy-occupied territory.

The King's Medal for Service in the Cause of Freedom was introduced to honour foreign civilians who had contributed in less dangerous roles to the British war effort, for example in fundraising activities.

1939–45 Star

This was awarded to all servicemen and women for any service between 3 September 1939 and 2 September 1945. Royal Navy personnel had to complete six months' service in hostile waters. Army personnel had to complete six months' service in an operational command. Airborne troops qualified if they had participated in any airborne operations or had completed two months in an operational unit. Merchant Navy qualified if they completed six months' service in hostile waters. Members of fighter aircraft crews who took part in the Battle of Britain (10 July–31 October 1940) were awarded a special Battle of Britain bar to this medal.

Atlantic Star

This star was awarded to those who served in the Battle of the Atlantic between 3 September 1939 and 8 May 1945. Royal and Merchant Navy, as well as army and RAF personnel serving with the navy, had to complete a minimum of six months' service in the Atlantic, home waters, north Russian convoys or the south Atlantic. RAF air crews had to complete two months' service in active operations within the specified area.

Air Crew Europe Star

This medal was awarded for operational flying from the UK over Europe between 3 September 1939 and 5 June 1945. RAF air crew had to complete a minimum of two months' service. Army personnel qualified if they served on air crew duties for four months.

Africa Star

This medal was awarded for a minimum of one day's service in North Africa between 10 June 1940 and 12 May 1943. Royal and Merchant Navy qualified through service in the Mediterranean. Service in the campaigns in Abyssinia, Somaliland and Eritrea between 10 June 1940 and 27 September 1941 would also qualify. In addition, Merchant Navy could qualify with service in operations in hostile waters off the Moroccan coast between 8 November 1942 and 12 May 1943. There were three additional clasps available for this medal: 8th Army, 1st Army and North Africa 1942–43.

☿ Pacific Star

This medal was awarded for service in the Pacific Theatre between 8 December 1941 and 2 September 1945. Members of the Royal and Merchant Navy had to serve in the Pacific Ocean, South China Sea and the Indian Ocean to qualify for this medal, providing that the six months' service for the 1939–45 medal had already been undertaken. Army personnel had to serve in those territories that had been subjected to enemy or allied invasions. RAF crews had to complete at least one operational sortie over the area.

☿ Burma Star

This medal was awarded for service in the Burma Campaign between 11 December 1941 and 2 September 1945. Royal and Merchant Navy personnel qualified through service in an area that stretched between the Bay of Bengal, the southern-most point of Ceylon (now Sri Lanka), the southern-most point of Sumatra, and the western side of the Sunda Strait including the Malacca Straits. Army personnel qualified through service in any part of Burma between 11 December 1941 and 2 September 1945. RAF aircrew had to make one operational sortie in the area, while RAF ground crew had the same restrictions as the army.

If a serviceman qualified for both the Burma and Pacific Stars, they would be awarded the first gained star and add a clasp for the other earned star.

Italy Star

This medal was awarded for operational service in Sicily or Italy during the period 11 June 1943 to 8 May 1945. Royal and Merchant Navy service in the Mediterranean and the Aegean Sea, and operations in and around the Dodecanese, Corsica, Greece, Sardinia and Yugoslavia after 11 June 1943, would also qualify. Army personnel had no prior time qualification nor did RAF personnel.

France and Germany Star

This medal was awarded for service in France, Belgium, Holland or Germany between 6 June 1944 and 8 May 1945. Royal and Merchant Navy qualification had no prior time qualification. The qualifying service area was the direct support of land operations in France, Belgium, Holland and Germany; in the North Sea south of a line from the Firth of Forth to Kristiansand; in the English Channel; or in the Bay of Biscay east of longitude 6°W. Service off the coast of southern France qualified for the Italy Star. Shore-based naval personnel were subject to the same qualification as the army. Army personnel had to take part in any operation on land, and RAF aircrew had to take part in an operation sortie over Europe.

Defence Medal

Awarded for service in the forces, Civil Defence and Home Guard in non-operational areas subjected to air attack for at least three years, and for non-operational service in the forces overseas or outside the country of residence for at least one year.

 War Medal

This medal was awarded to all full-time personnel of the armed forces, and operational and non-operational service of at least twenty-eight days. The Merchant Navy requirement stated that a minimum of twenty-eight days should be served at sea.

Children Go to War – Boy Soldiers

'Does your mother know that you're out?' The military life can sometimes look very glamorous to those left at home. When this is combined with the kind of unbridled patriotism and jingoist propaganda that was common on all sides during the war years, it's not surprising that many young men were inclined to lie about their age and sign up. The minimum age for service in the British army was 18, while the US army would accept recruits from 17 with parental consent. Here are some of the youngest serving soldiers:

Reginald Earnshaw – Lied about his age to join the Merchant Navy, claiming he was 15 (the minimum age to enlist). He was in fact just 14 years and 152 days old when he was killed by a German aircraft attack in 1941.

Calvin Graham – Joined the US navy at age 12 in 1942. He was wounded at the Battle of Guadalcanal, while serving aboard the USS *South Dakota*. It was not combat but a fall from a pier which later crippled Graham.

Jack Lucas – In 1942 Lucas used his muscular build and height (5ft 8in) to enlist in the Marine Corps Reserve. He gave his age as 17 but was in fact just 14 years of age. He went on to be the youngest ever recipient of the Medal of Honour for his actions during the Iwo Jima Campaign.

James Clark – Tall for his age, Clark told the draft board he was 18 and became a paratrooper at 13. He went through basic training and served for a year before being discovered and dismissed. He finally got to Berlin in 1947, when he re-enlisted in the army aged 17.

It is worth noting that other nations did not share the British and American age restrictions for their combatants. Soviet armies certainly included boys of 16 and younger, while towards the end of the war the embattled Nazi state drew on the Hitler Youth to put boys as young as 12 into the field.

Evil in the Dock – The Nuremberg Trials

The Nuremberg Trials were a series of military tribunals held at the end of the war, in which prominent political, military, and economic leaders from Nazi Germany were prosecuted for their activities during the hostilities. The trials were held at the Palace of Justice in the city of Nuremberg, Germany between 1945 and 1946.

The first and best known of these was the Trial of the Major War Criminals adjourned before the International Military Tribunal (IMT). Before the eyes of the world, twenty-four of the most important, captured Nazis came before a panel of British, American, Soviet and French judges. The second set of trials of lesser war criminals was conducted under Control Council Law No. 10, at the US Nuremberg Military Tribunals (NMT). Below are the accused and their sentences:

- **Martin Bormann** – Nazi Party secretary: Sentenced to death in absentia.
- **Karl Dönitz** – Leader of the Kriegsmarine from 1943 and President of Germany: Sentenced to ten years' imprisonment.
- **Hans Frank** – Reich Law Leader 1933–45 and Governor-General of the General Government in occupied Poland: Sentenced to death.
- **Wilhelm Frick** – Hitler's Minister of the Interior 1933–43 and Reich Protector of Bohemia-Moravia 1943–45: Sentenced to death.
- **Hans Fritzsche** – Popular radio commentator and head of the news division of the Nazi Propaganda Ministry: Acquitted.
- **Walther Funk** – Hitler's Minister of Economics: Sentenced to life imprisonment.
- **Hermann Goering** – Reichsmarschall, Commander of the Luftwaffe 1935–45, chief of the 4-Year Plan 1936–45 and original head of the Gestapo: Sentenced to death.
- **Rudolf Hess** – Hitler's Deputy Führer until he flew to Scotland in 1941 to broker peace with Great Britain: Sentenced to life imprisonment.

- **Alfred Jodl** – Wehrmacht Generaloberst and chief of the OKW's operations division: Sentenced to death.
- **Ernst Kaltenbrunner** – Chief of RSHA 1943–45: Sentenced to death.
- **Wilhelm Keitel** – Head of Oberkommando der Wehrmacht: Sentenced to death.
- **Gustav Krupp von Bohlen und Halbach** – CEO of Krupp AG 1912–45: Medically unfit for trial.
- **Robert Ley** – Head of DAF, the German Labour Front: Committed suicide before the trial began.
- **Baron Konstantin von Neurath** – Minister of Foreign Affairs 1932–38 and Protector of Bohemia and Moravia 1939–43: Sentenced to fifteen years' imprisonment.
- **Franz von Papen** – Chancellor of Germany in 1932, Vice-Chancellor under Hitler 1933–34, ambassador to Austria 1934–38 and ambassador to Turkey 1939–44: Acquitted.
- **Erich Raeder** – Commander-in-chief of the Kriegsmarine 1928–43: Sentenced to life imprisonment.
- **Joachim von Ribbentrop** – Ambassador-Plenipotentiary 1935–36, ambassador to the United Kingdom 1936–38 and Nazi Minister of Foreign Affairs 1938–45: Sentenced to death.
- **Alfred Rosenberg** – Racial theory ideologist and Minister of the Eastern Occupied Territories 1941–45: Sentenced to death.
- **Fritz Sauckel** – Gauleiter of Thuringia 1927–45, Plenipotentiary of the Nazi slave-labour program 1942–45: Sentenced to death.
- **Dr Hjalmar Schacht** – President of the Reichsbank 1923–30 and 1933–38, and Economics Minister 1934–37: Acquitted.
- **Baldur von Schirach** – Head of the Hitlerjugend 1933–40 and Gauleiter of Vienna 1940–43: Sentenced to twenty years' imprisonment.

- **Arthur Seyss-Inquart** – Austrian Chancellor 1938, deputy leader in Poland 1939–40 and Reich Commissioner of the occupied Netherlands 1940–45: Sentenced to death.
- **Albert Speer** – Minister of Armaments 1942–45: Sentenced to twenty years' imprisonment.
- **Julius Streicher** – Gauleiter of Franconia 1922–40: Sentenced to death.

The Cost of War – UK Munitions Factories

Primarily built in the rearmament period in the run-up to the war, between 1934 and 1939, Royal Ordnance Factories (ROFs) were the UK government's munitions factories. Most of the ROFs were deliberately built away from London (which was considered at risk from bombing) and were largely self-contained with their own coal-fired power stations and on-site facilities. They fell into three main types – Engineering, Filling and Explosives – though other installations also specialised in small arms and rifles. Below is a list of the facilities that kept our forces armed and dangerous:

Royal Arsenal (Factory No. 1)
Royal Small Arms (Factory No. 2)
Royal Powder Mill (Factory No. 31)
ROF Aycliffe (Filling Factory No. 8)
ROF Birtley

- ROF Bishopton (Explosive ROF)
- ROF Blackburn
- ROF Blackpool (SAA Factory)
- ROF Brackla (Filling Factory No. 11)
- ROF Bridgend (Filling Factory No. 2)
- ROF Bridgwater (Explosive ROF No. 37)
- ROF Burghfield (Filling Factory No. 18)
- ROF Cardiff (Engineering ROF)
- ROF Chorley (Filling Factory No. 1)
- ROF Dalmuir (Engineering ROF)
- ROF Drigg (Explosive ROF)
- ROF Dunham on the Hill (Explosives storage depot)
- ROF Elstow (Filling Factory No. 16)
- ROF Fazakerley (Rifles Factory)
- ROF Featherstone (Filling Factory No. 17)
- ROF Glascoed (Filling Factory No. 3)
- ROF Hereford
- ROF Hirwaun
- ROF Irvine (Explosive ROF)
- ROF Kirkby (Filling Factory No. 7)
- ROF Leeds (Engineering ROF)
- ROF Maltby (Rifles Factory)
- ROF Newport (Engineering ROF)
- ROF Nottingham (Engineering ROF)
- ROF Patricroft (Shop Engineering ROF)
- ROF Pembrey (Explosive ROF)
- ROF Poole (Engineering ROF)
- ROF Queniborough (Filling Factory No. 10)
- ROF Radway Green (SAA Factory No. 13)
- ROF Ranskill (Explosive ROF)
- ROF Risley (Filling Factory No. 6)

- ROF Sellafield
- ROF Southall (SAA Filling Factory)
- ROF Summerfield (SAA Filling Factory)
- ROF Spennymoor (SAA Factory)
- ROF Steeton (SAA Factory)
- ROF Swynnerton (Filling Factory No. 5)
- ROF Theale (Engineering ROF)
- ROF Thorp Arch (Filling Factory No. 9)
- ROF Wrexham (Explosive ROF)

Best War Books

The appetite amongst the reading public for books about the Second World War has kept authors, biographers and historians consistently busy since 1945. Even today, books about the war regularly appear in the bestseller lists. It would be impossible to provide an exhaustive list of noteworthy titles on the subject, but here are a few that we consider worth finding some space on your bookshelf for:

 History

Alan Clark, *Barbarossa … The Russian German Conflict 1941–45*
Alfred Price, *The Last Year of the Luftwaffe*
Antony Beevor, *Stalingrad and Berlin: The Downfall 1945*
William Shirer, *The Rise and Fall of the Third Reich*

Len Deighton, *Blitzkrieg: From the Rise of Hitler to the Fall of Dunkirk*
Max Hastings, *Overlord: D-Day and the Battle for Normandy*
Max Hastings, *Armageddon: The Battle for Germany, 1944–1945*
Max Hastings, *Retribution: The Battle for Japan, 1944–45*
John Toland, *The Rising Sun, 1936–1945*
John Keegan, *The Second World War*
Andrew Roberts, *The Storm of War: A New History of the Second World War*

 Biography
Ian Kershaw, *Hitler*
Roy Jenkins, *Churchill: A Biography*
Conrad Black, *Franklin Delano Roosevelt: Champion of Freedom*
David Fraser, *Knight's Cross: A Life of Field Marshal Erwin Rommel*
Robert Dallek, *Harry S. Truman*
Jonathan Fenby, *The General: Charles de Gaulle*
Elmer B. Potter, *Nimitz*
Robert Self, *Neville Chamberlain: A Biography*
Herbert P. Bix, *Hirohito and the Making of Modern Japan*
Richard Breitman, *The Architect of Genocide: Himmler and the Final Solution*

 Memoirs
Winston Churchill, *The Second World War*
Albert Speer, *Inside The Third Reich*
Viscount Montgomery of Alamein, *The Memoirs of Field Marshal Montgomery*
Admiral Karl Doenitz, *Memoirs: Ten Years And Twenty Days*
Arthur Harris, *Bomber Offensive*

Personal Narratives

Guy Sajer, *The Forgotten Soldier*

Eugene Sledge, *With The Old Breed* (US marine memoir)

Stephen E. Ambrose, *Band of Brothers*

Studs Terkel, *The Good War: An Oral History of World War II*

Peter White, *With the Jocks*

Richard E. Overton, *God Isn't Here*

Paul Brickhill, *Reach for the Sky: Story of Douglas Bader, D.S.O., D.F.C.*

Ron Werneth, *Beyond Pearl Harbour: The Untold Stories of Japan's Naval Airmen*

Anne Frank, *The Diary of a Young Girl*

Robert Leckie, *Helmet for My Pillow*

The Cost of War – Top Military Blunders

The Defence of the Philippines

In the spring of 1942, General Douglas MacArthur decided to draw a line in the sand against the advancing Japanese forces and attempted to defend the entire Philippine archipelago. The vastness of the area meant US troops were spread thinly, and required supplies of food and ammunition to be scattered throughout the islands in the hope of supporting this widely disparate force. The venture was doomed from the start and

MacArthur's men were quickly driven back to into the Bataan Peninsula. Here, over 76,000 American and Filipino troops were starved into surrendering by the encircling Japanese over four painful months.

The Liberation of the Philippines

Hubris rarely aids good military judgement, and MacArthur had not taken his humiliation in the Philippines well. By 1944 he was back and determined to retake the islands. In reality, Japanese air and ground forces right across the Pacific were now in decline, and those in the Philippines were doubly vulnerable as they were isolated from the main body of Japanese forces. A series of daring amphibious landings faced fanatical Japanese resistance, but the Allied forces eventually prevailed. In the wider scheme of an ultimate assault on the Japanese mainland the action had little tactical value, however. That is, beyond a photo opportunity as General MacArthur triumphantly waded ashore at Leyte – a moment which, arguably, served to extend the war by several months.

The Maginot Line

Following the First World War, France set about creating an impenetrable line of fixed defences on its border with Germany, called the Maginot line. With its gun emplacements, concrete bunkers and underground supply system it was indeed impressive; the problem was it simply didn't reach all the way to the coast. This presented a 100-mile-wide gap which any attacker could simply drive through to outflank the French defenders. Sure enough, in the spring of 1940 the ultra mobile German blitzkrieg did just that, and in a matter of weeks had encircled and overpowered the British and French armies.

The Battle of Kursk

In July 1943 Hitler was largely in denial about the loss of the 6th Army in Stalingrad. Rather than recast his plans, he grew increasingly confident that he would be able to recreate some of the dramatic military coups of his early career. Despite the fact that the tide of war in Russia was clearly turning, he routinely forbade his generals from making tactical withdrawals and planned a mighty hammer-blow against the Soviets. He attempted that blow at Kursk, where he launched a massive offensive against a large and well-entrenched body of Soviet defenders. The massive concentration of force meant that the Soviet lines did bend but – unfortunately for Hitler – they didn't break. Furthermore, the Germans discovered they had driven into the world's largest tank trap, and the ensuing counter-attack consigned a huge portion of their army and air force on the Eastern Front to destruction.

Anzio Landings

As part of the re-conquest of Europe, 22 January 1944 saw American and British troops land virtually unopposed at Anzio on the Italian coast. Although resistance had been expected, on the day the invaders lost just thirteen troops in the operation. At this point, everyone expected the Allies to push on into the interior and ultimately to challenge nearby Rome. Instead, Major General John P. Lucas chose to turn down the offer of help to advance from Italian Resistance and consolidated his forces on the beachhead. This provided a golden opportunity for the Germans, under General Kesselring, to pour every available soldier into the area and begin a systematic counter-attack that would cost some 20,000 Allied lives. Lucas' refusal to move baffled both his men and Allied high command. As Churchill

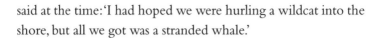

said at the time: 'I had hoped we were hurling a wildcat into the shore, but all we got was a stranded whale.'

The Italian Invasion of Greece and Egypt

Mussolini had big dreams of pulling his martial weight in his fascist partnership with Germany, and he planed to do it by rebuilding the Roman Empire. With this on his mind, he unleashed his oversized but inept army against Greece in the summer of 1940, whilst simultaneously attacking Egypt from Italian colonies in Libya. But, in both territories, local forces backed and trained by the British made short work of the Italian invaders, forcing Hitler to send in German reinforcements to stabilise his ally. The rear-guard action on Italy's behalf had a serious knock-on effect in Hitler's war effort, simultaneously removing vital troops from other campaigns and delaying his plans for the invasion of Russia.

The Blitz

The terrifying speed of the fall of France, and the collapse of British Expeditionary Force in June of 1940, meant that the UK was in real danger of a sea-borne invasion by German forces. Only the under-strength and overstretched RAF stood between English soil and Germany's unstoppable army. Initially, the Luftwaffe was doing a great job attacking British airfields and ammunition dumps. Indeed they nearly brought this last bastion of defence to it knees. But a small-scale RAF bomber raid on Berlin, on the night of 25 August 1940, so enraged Hitler that he ordered Goering to switch his aerial assault to civilian targets in London. In doing so, he gave the RAF a much needed chance to regroup and rearm, and solidified world opinion – particularly in America – against the German attack.

By August, a reinvigorated RAF would see off the Germans for good.

The Invasion of Russia

Hitler's plan to simultaneously defeat communism and enslave an inferior race on his own doorstep was arguably doomed as soon as he delayed the date of the invasion – a decision that inadvertently left his troops prey to the Russian winter. German soldiers, who had previously depended on speed and mobility to make swift gains on the battlefield, now found themselves bogged down in a three-year war of attrition against a power that matched them in commitment, had seemingly bottomless reserves of manpower and an immense industrial capability. The invasion also left Hitler fighting a war on two massive fronts across thousands of miles. After their defeat at Stalingrad in 1942 (see below), Germany was on the defensive and spent the rest of the war fighting a rear-guard action against the massive Soviet force that eventually ransacked Berlin.

Pearl Harbor

The surprise attack on the American naval bases at Pearl Harbor in 1941 was a well-planned and executed operation that seemed to result in a daring and spectacular victory for Japan. In fact, it would sow the seeds for their eventual defeat. The reality was that Japanese pilots succeed in sinking largely obsolete battleships (many of which were cannibalised for parts or raised); they also failed to knock out the major infrastructure on the island, which meant that the Americans could continue to use Pearl Harbor as their forward base of operations in the Pacific during the war. The attack brought a highly motivated America into the war and gave them the spur required to update

their fleet, which, by the end of the conflict, would be vastly technologically superior to Japan's. Most crucially, the Japanese failed to sink any American aircraft carriers and these would prove decisive in the final outcome of the Battle of the Pacific.

Dunkirk

Having effortlessly overrun the combined British and French armies in northern France and Belgium in June of 1940, the German army were in an ideal position to deliver a fatal blow to the Allies. However, Hitler – still hopeful of a pact with a Britain that he felt was closely aligned with Germany's Aryan heritage – halted his armies just miles short of the coast and forfeited a conclusive victory. Over the next few days, more than 300,000 British and French soldiers were evacuated to England in a rag-tag fleet of naval and civilian vessels. Had they not been evacuated, it is doubtful the British army could have ever recovered and certainly could not have mounted any kind of defence against the Germans and Italians in North Africa the following year.

Stalingrad

Arguably the battle which cost Germany victory in the war, Stalingrad remains one of military history's greatest blunders. Hitler's plan to seize the oil-rich Caucasus region of the Soviet Union, in the summer of 1942, ground to a halt when he allowed the main body of his army to become diverted by an attack on the city named after the Soviet leader Joseph Stalin. Both dictators felt that the symbolic nature of Stalingrad meant the battle must be won at any cost. The result was months of savage conflict within the bombed-out ruins of the city, which left hundreds of thousands dead on both sides. Despite dominating 90 per cent of the territory in the early stages of the battle, Field Marshal Von Paulus, forbidden to retreat or breakout, eventually found his exhausted and under-supplied army entirely surrounded and was forced to surrender over 250,000 men in February 1943. Stalingrad meant Hitler lost his chance to secure a vital supply of oil, and that the myth of the Wehrmacht's invincibility was finally destroyed.

Fleeing the Storm – War Criminals on the Run

At the end of war, a series of trials were held to bring to justice those who had committed atrocities during the conflict. As well as the highly publicised show trials of Nazi leaders at Nuremburg, there was an International Military Tribunal in the Far East and individual trials for actions in particular countries or by particular groups. Despite this work, many war criminals slipped the net. Some were given sanctuary in the Soviet Union in exchange for their skills, others fled to South American (and particularly Argentina) and many simply integrated back into society under assumed names. Despite the passage of time, they are still considered fugitives. Below is the list of the most wanted, as defined by the Simon Wiesenthal Centre:

- **Alois Brunner** – Believed to be living in Syria, he was an operative of Adolf Eichmann and was responsible for the deportation of

Jews from Austria, Greece, France and Slovakia to Nazi death camps.

- **Aribert Heim** – Heim was a doctor in the Sachsenhausen, Buchenwald and Mauthausen death camps. He is charged with performing horrific experiments on camp inmates.
- **Klaas Carl Faber** – Faber volunteered for the Dutch SS and served in the SD as a member of the Sonderkommando Feldmeijer execution squad, which executed members of the Dutch resistance and those hiding Jews. Despite being convicted in Holland, he is now resident in Germany.
- **Gerhard Sommer** – Now resident in Germany, Sommer was a former SS-Untersturmführer in the 16th Panzergrenadier Division Reichsführer-SS. He participated in the massacre of 560 civilians in the Italian village of Sant'Anna di Stazzema.
- **Adam Nagorny** – Nagorny served as an SS guard at the Trawniki SS training camp and at the Treblinka I concentration camp where prisoners were used to build the nearby Treblinka death camp. He is now resident in Germany.
- **Milivoj Asner** – Now living in Austria, Asner served as police chief of Slovonska Ponega, Poland and played an active role in the persecution, deportation and murder of hundreds of Serbs, Jews and gypsies.
- **Sandor Kepiro** – Now living in Hungary, Kepiro served as a Hungarian policeman and is accused of the mass murder of 1,200 civilians in Novi Sad, Serbia.
- **Mikhail Gorshkow** – Believed to be living in Estonia after being denaturalised and deported from the US, Gorshkow participated in the murder of Jews in Belarus.
- **Soeren Kam** – Kam participated in the murder of anti-Nazi Danish newspaper editor Carl Henrik Clemmensen. Kam also stole the citizen registry of the Danish Jewish community and

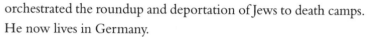

orchestrated the roundup and deportation of Jews to death camps. He now lives in Germany.

- **Karoly (Charles) Zentai** – Zentai participated in manhunts, persecution, deportation and murder of Jews in Budapest. Discovered living in Australia in 2004, Zentai is appealing his extradition to Hungary.
- **Algimantas Dailide** – Dailide arrested Jews who were then murdered by Nazis and Lithuanian collaborators. He immigrated to the US but was deported back to Germany where he now lives.
- **Ivan (John) Kalymon** – Kalymon served in Nazi-controlled Ukrainian Auxiliary Police in Lvov (in what was then Poland but is now Ukraine) where he participated in the murder and deportation of Jews living in the Lvov Ghetto. He now lives in the US.

Dates of Surrender of Axis Powers

As the tide of the war turned in favour of the Allies after 1943, one by one Axis forces were driven to capitulation across the world. Below are some of the key dates on the road to victory:

[i] 1943

| 31 January | German 6th Army surrenders at Stalingrad. |

[i] 1944

| 12 May | Surrender of Axis forces in North Africa. |
| 4 November | Surrender of Axis forces in Greece. |

ⓘ 1945

1 May	German forces in Italy surrender.
2 May	German forces in Berlin surrender.
4 May	German forces in Holland, Denmark and north-west Germany surrender.
	German forces in Bavaria surrender.
5 May	German forces in the 'fortress' city of Breslau surrender.
	German forces in the Channel Islands surrender.
7 May	Germany's unconditional surrender signed by Generals Jodl and Keitel in Reims.
8 May	VE (Victory in Europe) Day celebrated in west Europe.
9 May	VE Day celebrated in Russia.
15 August	Japan surrenders. The emperor's recorded speech to the nation announcing the end of the war is broadcast at 12 noon Japanese standard time.
2 September	Formal surrender of Japan signed by Shigemitsu (representing civil government) and General Unezu (representing the military) aboard the USS *Missouri* in Tokyo Bay.
2 September	VJ (Victory in Japan) Day celebrated.
7 September	Japanese forces in Shanghai surrender.
19 September	Remaining Japanese forces in China surrender.
12 September	Japanese forces in Singapore surrender.
13 September	Japanese forces in Burma surrender.
16 September	Japanese forces in Hong Kong surrender.

Despite the signing of a formal instrument of surrender, the war with Germany did not diplomatically end until 1951, when an end to the state of war with Germany was declared by the US Congress.

Some Japanese forces also refused to surrender, especially those marooned on small Pacific islands who had not heard about the end of hostilities, or feared that the radio broadcasts of the declaration of surrender were simply propaganda. Others simply chose to fight to the death. Serving Japanese combatants Hiroo Onoda and Teruo Nakamura emerged from hideouts in the Philippines and Indonesia as late as 1974.

Visit our website and discover thousands of
other History Press books.

www.thehistorypress.co.uk